RECOGNITION AND ENFORCEMENT OF CROSS-BORDER INSOLVENCY

A GUIDE TO INTERNATIONAL PRACTICE

Wiley Series in
COMMERCIAL LAW

Kaye/Methods of Executing Orders and Judgments in the UK
and Europe
0-471-94029-1 376 Pages

Rajak/European Corporate Insolvency – A Practical Guide
0-471-95239-7 952 Pages

Schoen/The French Stock Exchange:
A Practical Guide for Investors and Advisers
0-471-95550-7 310 Pages

Cooper/Recognition and Enforcement of Cross-Border Insolvency:
A Guide to International Practice
0-471-96310-0 150 Pages

Brown/Corporate Rescue
0-471-95237-0 700 Pages

Forthcoming titles

Dine/Eastern European Company Law
0-471-95281-8 400 Pages mid 1996

Pünder, Volhard, Weber & Axster/German Limited Liability Company
0-471-96581-2 350 Pages late 1996

Titles of related interest

INSOL/INSOL International Membership Directory
0-471-96179-5 230 Pages

Journal/International Insolvency Review
1800-518 Volume 5 2 issues per year

RECOGNITION AND ENFORCEMENT OF CROSS-BORDER INSOLVENCY

A GUIDE TO INTERNATIONAL PRACTICE

Neil Cooper FCCA FSPI FIPA

Partner, National Head of Corporate Recovery
at Robson Rhodes, Chartered Accountants, London
Vice President of INSOL and the AEPPC

and

Rebecca Jarvis LLB

Associate, Dibb Lupton Broomhead, Solicitors, London

Researcher: Sonali Abeyratne LLM (Lond.)
London School of Economics

Published in conjunction with INSOL International

JOHN WILEY & SONS
Chichester · New York · Brisbane · Toronto · Singapore

Published in 1996 by John Wiley & Sons Ltd,
Baffins Lane, Chichester,
West Sussex PO19 1UD, England

National   01243 779777
International   (+44) 1243 779777
e-mail (for orders and customer service enquiries): cs-books@wiley.co.uk
Visit our Home Page on http://www.wiley.co.uk
or http://www.wiley.com

Other Wiley Editorial Offices

John Wiley & Sons Inc., 605 Third Avenue,
New York, NY 10158-0012, USA

Jacaranda Wiley Ltd, 33 Park Road, Milton,
Queensland 4064, Australia

John Wiley & Sons (Canada) Ltd, 22 Worcester Road,
Rexdale, Ontario M9W 1L1, Canada

John Wiley & Sons (Asia) Pte Ltd, 2 Clementi Loop #02-01,
Jin Xing Distripark, Singapore 0512

Library of Congress Cataloging-in-Publication Data
Cooper, Neil H.
   Recognition and enforcement of cross-border insolvency: a guide to international
practice/by Neil Cooper and Rebecca Jarvis.
      p.   cm.— (Wiley series in commercial law)
   Published in conjunction with INSOL International.
   Includes bibliographical references.
   ISBN 0–471–96310–0
   1. Bankruptcy.   2. Conflict of laws—Bankruptcy.   I. Jarvis, Rebecca E.   II. Title.   III. Series.
K1375.C66   1966
340.9′78—dc20   96–22533
                                                                                  CIP

British Library Cataloguing Publication Data

A catalogue record for this book is available from the British Library

ISBN 0–471–96310–0

Typeset in 10/12pt Baskerville by Footnote Graphics, Warminster, Wilts
Printed and bound in Great Britain by Bookcraft (Bath) Ltd, Midsomer Norton, Somerset.

This book is printed on acid-free paper responsibly manufactured from sustainable forestation,
for which at least two trees are planted for each one used for paper production.

CONTENTS

INTRODUCTION

The economic benefits of increasing cross-frontier trade are now widely recognised, and it appears that political momentum around the world to break down
trade boundaries and create free trade areas is largely irreversible. However,
the development of a more global market-place has also led to an increase in
cross-frontier insolvency, either where the organisation concerned was doing
business in more than one jurisdiction or had trading partners in other countries. As a result, over the last 20 years there has been a developing debate on
the various national approaches to handling insolvency and a great deal of
effort has been put into attempts to reconcile the widely differing systems.

The unsuccessful attempt to develop a European Bankruptcy Convention in
the late 1970s and early 1980s was indicative of the problems that existed at an
international level. A widespread lack of understanding of the insolvency procedures of other nations was hardly surprising given the nuances of language used
and the historical background. In most European countries the current insolvency laws can be traced back to the 1860s. Since then court procedures and
general commercial practice have been used together to fill gaps and to make
the laws relevant to the twentieth century. There was, however, little concession
in that domestic legislation towards assistance for practitioners appointed in
other jurisdictions.

In the last 20 years, considerable efforts have been made to solve some of the
problems of access and recognition, prompted by the increasing number and
prominence of cross-border insolvencies. The climate for change was made
easier by the widespread recognition in the mid-to-late 1980s that insolvency
laws could be used constructively to rescue businesses and to save jobs, rather
than simply to conclude past failures. Notable examples of this were the United
States, with its infamous and widely misunderstood Chapter 11 provisions, and
the United Kingdom, where a security enforcement procedure (the appointment of a receiver and manager under a debenture) proved to be the most efficient and widely used insolvency procedure for saving businesses. However,

there is now the motivation worldwide to find constructive and efficient solutions for insolvent organisations, and this includes minimising the impact of differing national laws and practices where cross-border trading has taken place.

Not surprisingly, developments in cross-frontier insolvency have been monitored by INSOL since it was formed in 1982, and the subject has been a regular feature at its conferences. When the United Nations Commission for International Trade Law (UNCITRAL) expressed interest in the problems arising in this area, Insol was able to contribute the views of its members on how to develop solutions.

In April 1994, INSOL and UNCITRAL hosted a symposium for 90 representatives from 36 countries at UNCITRAL's headquarters in Vienna. Participants assessed the needs for cross-frontier co-operation, the steps that had been taken so far and ways in which the current position could be developed. Lord Hoffman, principal evaluator of the symposium, commented that:

> "the insolvency practitioners . . . are presented with an insolvent economic entity and their objective is to maximise the economic value of that entity for the benefit of the creditors, the employees and possibly even the shareholders . . . The primary objective in any kind of international co-operation, whether it be unilateral, treaty or general principle, is the need for efficient decision making in dealing with the insolvent entity."

Following that symposium, INSOL and UNCITRAL are jointly facilitating the development of judicial co-operation in insolvency matters, and the access and recognition of foreign practitioners and the proceedings under which they have been appointed. As part of this process, Insol established an Experts Committee which has produced what is believed to be the most thorough assessment to date of the position on international access and recognition.

Ron Harmer (Blake Dawson Waldron, Melbourne, Australia) and Evan Flaschen (Hebb & Gitlin, Hartford, Connecticut, United States) were the appointed reporters and worked with the Experts Committee of:

> Manfred Balz (Wilmer Cutler & Pickering, Berlin, Germany)
> Neil Cooper (Robson Rhodes, London)
> Professor Juan Dobson (University of Rosario, Argentina)
> Bruce Leonard (Cassels Brock & Blackwell, Toronto, Canada)
> The Hon Jean-Luc Vallens (Ministry of Justice, Paris, France)

This survey of cross-frontier recognition was produced as part of the report with the assistance of a large number of individuals around the world. The authors are particularly indebted to Mrs Sonali Abeyratne of the London School of Economics, Houghton Street, London WC2A 2AE, for her excellent research into the state of the law and practice in a large number of countries.

The authors sincerely hope that this publication is of use to practitioners. However, the survey was intended to assist in the preparation of a report rather than to create a definitive legal authority. Therefore, no liability can be accepted for the completeness or accuracy of the information on any country. Furthermore, since laws and attitudes change, insolvency practitioners and their advisers are urged to take appropriate local legal advice before deciding upon any particular course of action.

The authors would be extremely grateful to hear of any revisions, alternative interpretations or case law on the matters covered by this guide.

Terminology

The following short-form expressions have been used throughout:

"Foreign administrator" includes the holders of all manner of foreign insolvency appointments, be they as liquidator, trustee, administrator or any other title. Note that some countries will distinguish between court-appointed administrators and those appointed in out-of-court proceedings, such as the English administrative receivership. References to recognition should not be assumed automatically to include out-of-court proceedings.

"Foreign Administration" includes all types of insolvency proceedings without seeking to distinguish the method by which the foreign administrator was appointed.

"Bankruptcy" and "insolvency" have been used in their general usage meanings rather than their strict legal interpretations.

NEIL COOPER   REBECCA JARVIS
Robson Rhodes   *Dibb Lupton Broomhead*
London   *London*

April 1996

SOURCES OF INFORMATION AND BIBLIOGRAPHY

The information in this summary has been gleaned from a wide number of sources and checked with a large number of friends of Insol and the international organisations of the authors' firms. It is impossible to acknowledge all of those we have consulted without adding to the bulk of this document. We are particularly grateful, however, to the following, who have each contributed to a material extent the entry noted:

Argentina
Dr Juan M Dobson
Professor at Law
University of Rosario
Pellegrini 1270
Rosario 2000
Santa Fé

Australia
Ron Harmer
Blake Dawson Waldron
Level 39
101 Collins Street
Melbourne 3000

Dennis Cougle
Bent & Cougle Bentleys
332 St Kilda Road
Melbourne 3004

Austria
Professor Dr Walter H Rechberger
University of Vienna
Schottenbastei 10–16
1010 Wien
Vienna

Bermuda
Robin J Mayor and Christian Luthi
Conyers Dill & Pearman
PO Box HM 666
Clarendon House
Church Street
Hamilton HM CX

Canada
R Gordon Marantz QC
Osler Hoskin & Harcourt
1 First Canadian Place
PO Box 50
Toronto M5X 1B8

Canada (continued)
E Bruce Leonard
Cassels Brock & Blackwell
Scotia Plaza, Suite 2100
40 King Street West
Toronto M5H 3C2

Denmark
Ole Borch, Advokat
Berning Schlüter Hald
Bredgade 6
DK 1260 Copenhagen K

Lars Stanvig and Henril Andersen
Advokat
Bech, Brunn & Trolle
3 Nørre Farimagsgade
DK 1364 Copenhagen K

Egypt
M. Sabrey Heakal
McGladrey & Pullen
1440 Midwest Plaza West
801 Nicollect Avenue
Minneapolis 55402–2529
USA

France
Jean Luc Vallens
Judge in the French Court of Appeal
General Secretary
Institut du Droit Local Alsacien-Mosel-
lan
8 Rue des Farivains
67081 Strasbourg

Germany
Dr Manfred Balz
Wilmer Cutler & Pickering
Friedrichstrasse 95
D–10117 Berlin

Gibraltar
Isaac Marrache
Marrache & Co
PO Box 85
5 Cannon Lane
Gibraltar

Israel
Adv. Gideon Fisher
Zvi Tamir & Co
70 Hey Iyar Street
62198 Tel Aviv

Italy
Dott. Renato Viale
Procuratore Generale on.
Presso la Corte di Cassazione
Via S Nazaro 9D
16145 Genova

Japan
Hon Shinjiro Takagi, Judge
Tokyo District Court
23–14 Kugabara 1–chome
Ota-ku
Tokyo

Jersey
Michael Wilkins
The Viscount
Royal Court of Justice
Viscount's Department
27 Hill Street
St Helier
Jersey JE2 4UA

The Netherlands
Ronald de Ruuk, Advocaat
Stibbe Simont Monahan Duhot
Postbus 75640
1070 AP Amsterdam

New Zealand
Steve Dukeson and John G Robertson
Martelli McKegg Wells & Cormack
PO Box 5745
Auckland

Scotland
James M Arnott
MacRoberts
27 Melville Street
Edinburgh EH3 7JF

South Africa
Judge Ralph H Zulman
Supreme Court of South Africa
PO Box 10390
Gauteng
Johannesburg 2000

Spain
Fernando Pombo, Abogado
Gomez-Acebo & Pombo
Castellana 164
28046 Madrid

Sweden
Elisabet Fura-Sandström, Advokat
Vinge
Smålandsgatan 20
Box 1703
S-111 87 Stockholm

Switzerland
Dr Stephen V Berti, Attorney
Schraner & Berti
Weinbergstrasse 43
8006 Zurich

United States of America
Evan Flaschen, Attorney
Hebb & Gitlin
One State Street
Hartford
Conneticut 06103–3178

The principal written works relating to more than one country to which we have referred are:

Dennis Campbell, *Attacking Foreign Assets*
Richard A Gitlin and Rona Mears, *International Loan Workouts and Bankruptcies*
Harry Rajak and Gordon White, *A Practitioners' Guide to European Corporate Insolvency Law*
C Platto, *Enforcement of Foreign Judgments Worldwide* (1989)
E Bruce Leonard and Christopher W Besant, *Current Issues in Cross-Border Insolvency and Reorganisations*
D A Botwinik and K W Weinrib, *European Bankruptcy Laws* (2nd ed)
Dicey and Morris, *The Conflict of Laws* (11th ed)

Chapter 1

ARGENTINA

1. Under general law

There appears to be a positive approach to the recognition and enforcement of foreign judgments and judicial co-operation. Argentine courts do not appear to review the merits of foreign judgments or demand reciprocity. Foreign claimants will, however, experience restrictions when seeking to enforce foreign judgments in Argentina.

Argentine law distinguishes recognition from enforcement. Although all foreign judgments are recognised under Argentine law, only judgments that require a defendant to give, do, or stop doing something can be enforced, therefore orders which are of a declaratory nature may be recognised but they are not enforceable.

While the making of a foreign insolvency order is deemed to be an act of bankruptcy for the purpose of opening a "concurso" in Argentina, only the debtor or a local creditor may petition for that. Before insolvency proceedings may be commenced in Argentina on the strength of a foreign insolvency order, "exequatur" of the foreign insolvency order is essential. This requires the foreign order to:

- be final and have been made by a competent court recognised by the courts of Argentina. If the foreign court has jurisdiction according to its own law but not according to Argentine law, enforcement will be denied;
- have originated through due process and meet the standard of authenticity required by Argentine law;
- not contradict another decision of an Argentine court; and
- conform with Argentine public policy.

2.   Assisting legislation

There is no express recognition of foreign administrators or foreign insolvency proceedings embodied in Argentine statutes. Unless an international treaty applies, a foreign insolvency order is not directly enforceable as such in Argentina.

The right of a local creditor to petition on the grounds of a foreign bankruptcy order has been traced to the Hanover Procedure Ordinance 1850. It is an exceptional provision because Argentine insolvency law otherwise requires it to be proved in court that the debtor has defaulted in the payment of specific debts. Argentine law extends internationally in that an Argentine court can declare a transaction entered into by an Argentine national abroad void or voidable.

The Montevideo Private International Law Treaties of 1889 and 1940 lay down principles of unity and plurality in respect of insolvency proceedings in the signatory states. Relations between Peru, Bolivia, Paraguay, Uruguay and Argentina are governed by the 1889 treaty. Only Paraguay, Uruguay and Argentina have ratified the 1940 treaty. The law of the state where the proceedings are opened applies to those proceedings.

A foreign administrator appointed in one of the signatory states may take preventative measures over property located in other signatory states. His authority will be recognised in all states, not just the state where he was appointed. The court of the state whose co-operation is requested must advertise the opening of the bankruptcy in the requesting state and the preventative measures ordered there. Local creditors then have the option to petition for a separate parallel bankruptcy in the co-operating state.

If there are parallel bankruptcies, local creditors are paid in priority out of funds held in each jurisdiction and any remaining funds will be to the order of the court of the state where the other bankruptcy is proceeding. There is judicial co-operation to this end.

If there is a single bankruptcy, all creditors (local and otherwise) file their claims and prove their rights in accordance with the law of the state where the proceedings were opened.

3.   Insolvency practice

As regards the signatories to the Montevideo Private International Law Treaties of 1889 and 1940, there is fairly extensive judicial co-operation and recognition of foreign administrators.

There is no formal recognition of foreign administrators or insolvency proceedings opened in other jurisdictions, but because the Ley de Concursos 19.551, article 4 deems the making of a foreign insolvency order to be an act of insolvency in Argentina, the extra-territorial effect of the foreign insolvency order is arguably recognised (or at least capable of being recognised).

Furthermore, the *Panair do Bristol SA* case decided by the Argentine Supreme Court gives limited recognition in that it acknowledges that although Argentine courts will not recognise foreign insolvency proceedings they will co-operate with a foreign administrator to the extent that he is recognised as the agent of the debtor.

Prior to 1983, an agreement for the payment of a debt outside Argentina automatically subordinated the claim of the foreign creditor to the claims of local creditors in Argentine insolvency proceedings. The distinction between foreign and local is made, not on the basis of nationality but on the location agreed upon by the parties for the payment of the debt. The domicile of a debt is determined according to Argentine law, Civil Code articles 747–749 and Commercial Code, article 207. The Insolvency Reform Act 1983 (Ley 22.917) modified the rule so that now the subordination of a foreign creditor's claim takes place only in the event of plural insolvency proceedings. Foreign creditors subordinated in such circumstances still have the right to participate in Argentine insolvency proceedings but only to the extent that there are "remnant" funds from which they may be paid. Creditors whose debts are payable abroad are entitled to take part in Argentine insolvency proceedings only if they are not participating in any foreign proceedings.

In the event of insolvency proceedings only in Argentina, a foreign creditor can participate if he can prove that there would be reciprocity if an Argentine creditor asked to participate in proceedings in his jurisdiction.

Actions in respect of real property in Argentina are governed exclusively by Argentine law (Civil Code article 10). Therefore, any foreign judgment in respect of property situated in Argentina is not enforceable in Argentina because the court having jurisdiction in real property actions is the court where the property is situated.

4. Examples

Panair do Brazil SA Case

The bankruptcy judge of the Brazilian airline Panair do Brazil SA, requested the judicial co-operation of the court in Buenos Aires, Argentina for the sale of assets in Argentina. The Brazilian bankruptcy administrator appointed an agent in Buenos Aires, but the Argentine judge ruled that a Brazilian bankruptcy order had no effect in Argentina. The judge appointed a local administrator but did not order the opening of bankruptcy proceedings in Argentina. The Brazilian debtor then made two payments to creditors in Argentina.

The question before the Court of Appeal was whether the foreign debtor could make valid payments in Argentina. The Court held that as Panair was not bankrupt in Argentina, it could make valid payments under Argentine law provided there were no local creditors. However, it was necessary to open local bankruptcy proceedings to establish the existence of local creditors.

The Supreme Court decided that to recognise a foreign administrator would be a violation of the Argentine "ordre public".

The legal consequences of the *Panair* case can be summarised as follows:

- recognition of the powers of the foreign administrator violates Argentine internal public policy;
- violation only occurs when there are local creditors but if none appear, the agency of a foreign administrator may be recognised;
- an Argentine administrator **must** be appointed according to Argentine rules to determine whether there are local creditors; and
- the granting of a request by a foreign administrator for the sale of assets in Argentina will not include recognising him as such.

Swift de la Palata SA Case

The issue that arose was whether an American holding corporation was liable for debts of its wholly-owned subsidiary in Argentina and, as such, whether its wholly-owned subsidiaries with assets in Argentina were similarly liable. The Argentine Court held that such liability was possible.

Chapter 2

AUSTRALIA

1. Under general law

There are now three bases on which a judgment or other order of a foreign court may be recognised and enforced in Australia.

First, under the common law, Australia has always followed the doctrine of "comity" and subject to the application of the rules that have developed in that area, foreign judgments may be recognised and enforced under that regime.

Secondly, each of the states and territories of Australia has had legislation providing for the direct execution of foreign judgments. The principles of the legislation do not greatly depart from the common law rules but the legislation has been helpful by providing for a reasonably efficient procedure for "registration" of a foreign judgment and its subsequent enforcement.

Thirdly, the recent enactment of federal legislation, Foreign Judgments Act 1991 (FJA), largely supersedes the state and territory legislation mentioned above. The main advantage of this legislation is that it provides a "one stop" method of registration which then has effect throughout Australia (rather than, as has previously been the case under the state and territorial legislation, requiring acts of separate and distinct registration in each state or territory in which it might be sought to enforce the judgment). The FJA has also modernised the rules relating to recognition and enforcement.

The FJA applies to judgments and other orders of courts in a schedule of countries. In those countries, the registration process is almost automatic. In cases of non-scheduled countries, recognition and enforcement of the judgment may still be sought on common law principles.

Money judgments made by a superior foreign court may be registered in Australia's superior courts under the FJA. Australian courts will refuse registration if the foreign judgment was obtained by fraud, if it is contrary to Australian public policy or contravenes the enforcement legislation.

Once registered, the judgment will have the same force and effect as if it had originally been given by the registering court. A number of methods of enforcement are available, including warrants of execution and possession, the appointment of a receiver or liquidator or garnishee proceedings. A final foreign judgment must be obtained before the judgment can be registered in Australia but to protect assets, certain interim action may be taken; for example, a *Mareva* injunction may be granted pending the granting of a foreign judgment under some circumstances.

2.   Assisting legislation

The Bankruptcy Act 1966, section 29 and the Corporations Law 1991, section 581 specifically empower the Australian courts to "act in aid" and be auxiliary to foreign courts having insolvency jurisdiction. This is mandatory for the following "specified countries":

- Canada;
- Jersey;
- Malaysia;
- New Zealand;
- Papua New Guinea;
- Singapore;
- Switzerland;
- United Kingdom; and
- United States.

This assistance is discretionary for all other countries. The procedure involves a letter of request being issued from a foreign court requesting aid in an insolvency matter which is filed in the Australian court. The latter may exercise such power as it could have exercised if the situation had arisen in its own jurisdiction. (Conversely Australian courts may request a foreign court with insolvency jurisdiction to act in aid of them.)

There is also provision at section 350(14) of the Corporations Law for ancillary proceedings to be started in respect of a foreign company registered in Australia, if that company is dissolved or winding-up proceedings have been commenced against it in its country of domicile. The foreign liquidator can cause a liquidator to be appointed in Australia and ancillary winding-up proceedings to be commenced there.

If a foreign company is not registered in Australia, ancillary proceedings may not be commenced; instead winding-up proceedings must be commenced in the relevant Australian court and the foreign administrator will need to intervene in those proceedings.

3. Insolvency practice

The operation of the Australian insolvency laws (including those dealing with co-operation with and recognition of foreign administrators) is probably more sophisticated than any other country in the world. There are two main forms of co-operation and recognition in Australia:

- recognition of and assistance to a foreign administrator under the assisting legislation; and
- recognition of and enforcement of foreign judgments/orders under the FJA and general comity.

Foreign insolvency orders will be recognised in Australia provided that the orders are proved to have been made in the foreign jurisdiction and that the foreign jurisdiction was sufficiently connected with the insolvent person or company and was properly exercised. However, the foreign order is not directly enforceable in Australia; a concurrent order must be obtained under the procedures set out in the Bankruptcy Act 1966, section 29 and the Corporations Law 1991 section 581. The nature and extent of the aid is in the discretion of the Australian courts although aid is mandatary for the specified countries. The courts will be concerned that local creditors are not prejudiced and that Australian law is not contravened. The courts must act in a manner consistent with their jurisdiction conferred by Australian legislation.

If the foreign insolvency proceedings are recognised, the foreign administrator will be accorded recognition. However, in practice Australian courts commence ancillary proceedings and then appoint an Australian administrator to assist the foreign administrator. The ancillary proceedings give effect to the purpose of the principal winding-up and ensure that locally-situated assets are collected and passed to the foreign administrator. The administration following such recognition will be vested in the Australian administrator and the foreign administrator will exert claims, take control of, realise and deal with insolvency property acting by the Australian administrator. There is, of course, no bar to the foreign administrator taking direct action in respect of property situate in Australia by, for example, enforcing a foreign-money judgment.

Where bankruptcy proceedings pertaining to an individual have been commenced in a foreign jurisdiction, an Australian court will usually follow the rule established in the case of *Goetze & Sons* v *Aders, Preyer & Co* (1874, 2R 150, 12 Sc LR 12) and consider any subsequent bankruptcy adjudication in Australia incompetent.

Reservations have been expressed by the English Court of Appeal about the decision in *Goetze* (see *Re Artola Hermanos, ex parte Andre Chale*, [1890] 24 QBD 640) but other decisions have accepted this rule (see *Re Anderson* [1911] 1 KB 896 and *Re Temple* [1947] 1 Ch 345).

The rules of private international law applicable in Australia distinguish between moveable and immoveable property. Moveable property will generally vest in the foreign administrator but immoveable property will remain vested in the foreign insolvent individual or company despite the foreign insolvency proceedings. Therefore the foreign administrator will need to intervene with regard to immoveable property.

4. Examples

Ayers v *Evans* (1981) 39 ALR 129

The appellant was a resident of New Zealand where he had been declared bankrupt. He was entitled to the unadministered residuary estate of his father which was being administered in New South Wales. The High Court of New Zealand by letter requested the aid of the Federal Court to get the residuary of the estate remitted to New Zealand. More than half the debts of the appellant were due to the New Zealand revenue authorities.

On hearing an application made under the Bankruptcy Act, section 29 (see above) the Federal Court made an order whereby the official receiver was appointed receiver of the appellant's father's estate with powers to sell it and directions to remit the proceeds to the official receiver of the bankruptcy in New Zealand.

The Court of Appeal judges concluded that there was no doubt that aid which could be provided included the transfer of the applicant's interests to the official assignee, or the appointment of a receiver of it for the official assignee, and that the nature, extent and terms of the aid remained a matter for the discretion of the Court.

In response to the appellant's argument that the Court should not lend its assistance to obtain money for the payment of revenue debts owed to another state, the Court held that the rule that courts should not act to enforce a revenue claim by another state will not apply if a liquidator or official assignee seeks to get property which will in due course benefit ordinary creditors as well as the revenue authorities. The appeal was therefore dismissed.

Chapter 3

AUSTRIA

1. Under general law

The Austrian Bankruptcy Act (*Konkursordnung*) 1914, as amended, section 180 governs the recognition of foreign bankruptcy orders by reference to the Austrian Enforcement Act (*Exekutionsordnung*), 1886/79 sections 79–82 and 84. The requirements for the recognition are:

- The foreign procedure must qualify as bankruptcy proceedings under Austrian law. Bankruptcy proceedings are defined as civil law state proceedings for the administration of property to satisfy creditors proportionately where the assets are insufficient to discharge all debts.
- Reciprocity under either the terms of an international treaty or a declaration of the Government, which has to be published in the federal law gazette (*Bundesgesetzblatt* (BGBI)).

The Austrian court will consider the foreign bankruptcy declaration according to the foreign insolvency law and only serious defects would prevent the recognition of foreign courts. The following procedural requirements are:

- the jurisdiction of the court which issued the order has to be established. If jurisdiction is not established by international treaty, the foreign court has jurisdiction according to the "Austrian formula of jurisdiction", and if jurisdiction is established, Austrian law is applied to the facts in issue;
- the foreign court has to intend its declaration to have extra-territorial effect;
- the orders must be served personally;
- the bankruptcy declaration has to be final; and
- the order must not contravene Austrian "public order".

The court of first instance where the insolvent debtor has his domicile or place of business has jurisdiction to decide on recognition. The application for the enforcement of the foreign order can be made by the administrator or by creditors.

2.   Assisting legislation

Austria is a party to the following relevant bilateral treaties:

-   Belgium, BGBl 1975/385 (restricted to the insolvencies of merchants and commercial companies);
-   France, BGBl 1980/237;
-   Germany, BGBl 1985/233; and
-   Italy, BGBl 1990/44 (restricted to the insolvencies of merchants and commercial companies).

There is also a treaty of enforcement with Turkey (BGBl 1932/90) and a treaty of recognition and enforcement with Great Britain (BGBl 1962/224 in the version of BGBl 1971/453), but these do not refer to insolvency orders.

Jurisdiction is determined differently by each treaty. It is the court of the state where the debtor has his management or the company has its headquarters in Belgium and Italy; the debtor has the centre of his economic activity or the company has its headquarters in France; or the debtor has the centre of his economic activity, the headquarters, the ordinary residence or the establishment in Germany. If jurisdiction is established, only the treaty with Germany provides an automatic recognition of the declaration of bankruptcy. In all other cases it is necessary to examine whether Austrian public order is violated.

3.   Insolvency practice

There are limited practical examples of recognition of foreign bankruptcy orders. This is because general recognition does not exist—there is only implicit recognition in the course of civil litigation or because of a petition for enforcement of a foreign order.

4.   Examples

Oberster Gerichshof (Supreme Court) 26 November 1985, 5 Ob 322/85, EvBl 1986/166

A creditor with a claim against a debtor who had his habitual abode in Germany filed the bankruptcy petition before an Austrian court claiming that the debtor had property in the district of the Austrian court, namely the right to use the car of his parents who lived in the court's district and an interest in a limited partnership which had ceased to exist.

The court of first instance and the Court of Appeal dismissed the petition for lack of jurisdiction.

The Supreme Court decided that under the treaty between Germany and Austria, if a competent court of one state makes a bankruptcy order, the court of the other state cannot make a bankruptcy order. In this case the debtor had his ordinary residence in Germany, therefore the Austrian court had no jurisdiction to make a bankruptcy order.

Patentant (Patent Office) 17 November 1989, B 43/87 (A 9083177), ORI 1990, 250=PBI 1990, 193

A Swedish company applied for the assignment of an Austrian patent from a company in a bankruptcy where the assignment was signed by its Swedish administrator.

The Austrian Patent Office refused the request of the Swedish company to take notice of the assignment, holding that an administrator appointed in Sweden is not allowed to make dispositions relating to Austrian patents. There was no bilateral insolvency treaty between Austria and Sweden. Decisions of the foreign court (in this case: the appointment of the administrator) therefore had no effect in Austria and the Austrian patent remained under the control of the debtor.

Chapter 4

BERMUDA

1. Under general law

Bermuda is a colony of the United Kingdom and the courts and legal system are based on the English legal system. The rules of practice and procedure are therefore very similar to those of England.

In Bermuda the winding-up of companies is governed by the Companies Act 1981 (which is based upon the English Companies Act 1948). There is no separate bankruptcy court in Bermuda. Winding-up and bankruptcy are governed by the civil jurisdiction of the Supreme Court.

Foreign money judgments can be enforced under Bermudan law either under statute or common law.

Under the Judgments Reciprocal Enforcement Act 1958 (JRE) a foreign money judgment will be recognised and enforced by the Bermudan courts as if it had been originally obtained in Bermuda. The JRE follows the same procedure as the Foreign Judgments (Reciprocal Enforcement) Act 1933 of the United Kingdom.

The JRE applies to the following countries:

Bahamas, Barbados, British Guyana, Gibraltar, Grenada, Hong Kong, Leeward Islands, St Vincent, Jamaica, Nigeria, Dominica, St Lucia, The Capital Territory, New South Wales, The Northern Territory, Queensland, Tasmania, Western Australia, South Australia, Australian Antarctic Territory, Heard & McDonald Territory, Coral Sea Islands Territory, Territory of Ashmore and Cartier Islands.

A judgment which is not registrable under the JRE must be sued upon as a separate action on the basis that the foreign judgment is treated as evidence of a debt. A foreign money judgment will be recognised and enforced by the Bermudan Court as a debt against the judgment debtor where the judgment:

- was final and conclusive in the foreign court;
- was obtained in a court with jurisdiction over the debtor;
- was not obtained by fraud;
- was not in respect of taxes, fines or penalties;
- did not contravene the public policy of Bermuda and the rules of natural justice were observed in the foreign proceedings.

2. Assisting legislation

There are no specific provisions in Bermudan legislation which provide that a Bermudan court will recognise a foreign bankruptcy, save for the Bankruptcy Act 1989, section 144, which provides that the Bermudan court shall assist the court having bankruptcy jurisdiction in any part of the United Kingdom.

There is no provision under the companies legislation which specifically provides for assistance to a foreign administrator.

A foreign creditor may apply for the bankruptcy of an individual or for the winding-up of a company provided the creditor follows the procedures set out in the Bankruptcy Act 1989 and the Companies Act 1981, respectively.

3. Insolvency practice

Bermudan courts view as highly persuasive authority, English case law which prevailed prior to the enactment of the Insolvency Act 1986, section 426.

Bermudan courts will therefore tend to follow English common law in giving assistance to foreign administrators recognising both the existence of the foreign administrator and his title to moveable property situated in Bermuda.

In relation to the winding-up of a foreign company by a foreign court, however, a Bermudan court will hold that the winding-up does not effect an assignment of the assets to the administrator. The result is that whilst Bermudan courts will recognise a foreign administrator, there is no uniform approach as to the assistance the Bermudan courts will give a foreign administrator.

4. Examples

None available.

Chapter 5

CANADA

1. Under general law

Canadian law generally is based on English common law, except in the province of Quebec where the legal system traces its origins to eighteenth century French civil law.

The provinces tend to have the predominant legislative jurisdiction over creditors' and debtors' rights and remedies pre-bankruptcy, including credit and security transactions, whilst the federal government, through its bankruptcy and insolvency jurisdiction, tends to be predominant in regulating the rights and remedies of creditors where a debtor has become insolvent.

The Reciprocal Enforcement of Judgments Act 1967 (the "Act") provides a national standard for the recognition and enforcement of foreign-money judgments. Alberta, British Columbia, Manitoba, Newfoundland, Nova Scotia, Prince Edward's Island and Yukon Territory have adopted this Act; whereby each province provides for limited reciprocity in recognition and enforcement of "foreign" judgments obtained in or outside Canada. The other provinces and territories have also adopted the Act, but only in respect of judgments obtained within Canada. In addition, most provinces have adopted the Canada-United Kingdom Treaty for the recognition and enforcement of judgments.

A foreign-money judgment can be enforced in Canada after it is registered with a local court. Once registered, a foreign judgment has the same force and effect as if it were a judgment given in Canadian proceedings.

The common law rules provide, as a minimum, that a foreign judgment is not enforceable in Canada if it:

- appears to have been obtained by fraud;
- is for the payment of a penalty under foreign law;
- may be challenged on the basis that the proceedings in which it was obtained are contrary to natural justice;

- purports to enforce directly, or indirectly, revenue laws of another country; or
- is, in the original cause of action, contrary to Canadian public policy.

The status and capacity of foreign administrators will be recognised if they have been appointed in foreign insolvency proceedings recognised by the Canadian courts and which do not contravene Canadian concepts of natural justice. There is no need to register a bankruptcy order in Canada to allow a foreign administrator to act. If the foreign administrator has difficulties, he can apply to the Canadian courts for assistance; that is recognition of his status and his rights to the assets. A foreign court-appointed receiver will only be recognised if a sufficient connection between the debtor and the court appointing the receiver is proved.

Once the courts recognise the foreign administrator, they will also recognise his authority to commence and defend proceedings in Canada. Canadian courts recognise the effect of foreign insolvency proceedings on moveables in Canada if there are no competing domestic claims and if the foreign jurisdiction rendering the bankruptcy order has a substantial connection with the bankrupt. Sufficient connection would be seen if:

- the bankrupt is domiciled in the jurisdiction of the foreign court;
- the bankrupt conducts his main business in the foreign jurisdiction; and
- the bankrupt submits to the jurisdiction of the foreign court making the bankruptcy order.

If the bankrupt is a corporate entity, Canadian courts will not recognise the authority of a foreign administrator unless he was appointed either under the laws of the place of incorporation of the bankrupt or under the laws of a jurisdiction with which the bankrupt has a substantial connection.

If the foreign insolvency proceedings and the foreign administrator are recognised, the assignment of the bankrupt's moveable property situate in Canada will be automatically recognised, provided that the law governing the foreign insolvency proceedings provides for the property of the bankrupt to be vested in the foreign administrator. The foreign administrator must apply to the Canadian courts for authority to enforce his rights over immoveable property.

In Quebec, the existence of a civil law code may also have some impact. Foreign insolvency proceedings will generally not be recognised if the court considers the rights of local creditors will be adversely affected. Foreign administrators who are recognised by the laws of Quebec also have the right to bring proceedings in Quebec.

2. Assisting legislation

The three principal Canadian Insolvency Acts; the Bankruptcy and Insolvency Act 1949 (as amended 1970), the Companies Creditors Arrangements Act 1970 and the Winding-Up Act 1970, apply equally to common law provinces and to Quebec. There are no statutory provisions that govern the recognition of, and co-operation with, foreign insolvency proceedings by Canadian courts.

Canada is not a party to any bilateral or multilateral treaty dealing with insolvency matters.

3. Insolvency practice

The climate in Canada for judicial co-operation in international insolvencies is becoming increasingly favourable.

Although the statutes are silent on judicial co-operation, Canadian courts sitting in bankruptcy proceedings have assisted or co-operated when similar proceedings have been commenced, or have been pending in, a foreign jurisdiction through, for example, the exercise of their discretion to stay or refuse local proceedings.

The courts have, however, demonstrated a reluctance to send Canadian creditors to other jurisdictions to pursue their remedies where they may be prejudiced. Since recognition of a foreign bankruptcy order does not preclude the Canadian courts making a bankruptcy order against the debtor (see *Re E H Clarke & Co* v *Royal Bank* (1922) 3 C BR 593.), in such situations the courts have encouraged commencing concurrent proceedings in Canada to address the Canadian assets. A court may also restrain a Canadian creditor from making a claim in a foreign bankruptcy to prevent the creditor from obtaining an advantage (*Pitts* v *Hill & Hill Truck Line, Inc* (1987) 66 CBR (NS) 273).

As a general rule, all foreign claims, except revenue claims, are provable in a Canadian bankruptcy, whether or not the debt upon which the claim is based is governed by local or foreign law. In one case, a revenue claim was recognised on the basis that the Canadian estate would have been unjustly enriched at the expense of the revenue authority making the claim and it would have been inequitable not to recognise the claim (*Re Sefel Geographical Ltd* (1989) 70 CBR (NS) 97).

A creditor need not reside or carry on business in Canada and the provable claim need not have arisen in Canada. Foreign creditors, like domestic creditors, are simply required to prove their claims by completing proofs of claim in the prescribed form.

Priorities given under Canadian law to classes of creditors apply to Canadian and foreign creditors; priorities granted to an unsecured creditor by the law of a foreign jurisdiction are not recognised in Canada. Generally, Canadian law will recognise creditors having security over foreign assets if the security is properly perfected under the law where the assets are located.

Further, although there are a few cases to the contrary, the general rule appears to be that foreign administrators cannot independently impeach antecedent transactions occurring in Canada, or which result in the debtor's assets being vested in a third party (*Galbraith* v *Grimshaw [1910] AC 508*).

4. Examples

Olympia & York Developments Ltd v Royal Trust Co (1993) 20 CBR (3d) 165

In the case of Olympia & York Developments Ltd, the company's assets included major real estate developments in Toronto, New York and London which led to concurrent bankruptcy proceedings in Canada, the United States and England.

In dealing with a United States affiliate, the parties negotiated a protocol between themselves in order to harmonise the matters arising under the Companies' Creditors Arrangement Act 1970 and United States Chapter 11 proceedings.

The protocol dealt with issues concerning the corporate governance of various corporate parties that held assets directly or indirectly in United States real estate. The parties applied to the Ontario court for its approval of the protocol. Blair J, approving the protocol, stated:

"The courts of the various jurisdictions should seek to co-operate amongst themselves, in my view, in facilitating the trans-border resolution of such disputes as a whole, where that can be done in a fashion consistent with their own fundamental principles of jurisprudence. The interests of international co-operation and comity, and the interests of developing at least some degree of certitude in international business and commerce, call for nothing less".

Re IIT (1975) 19 CBR (NS) 263

The Supreme Court of Ontario recognised the status of liquidators appointed under the laws of Luxembourg and ordered the assets belonging to the bankrupt, and located in Ontario, to be vested in the foreign liquidators for distribution to creditors in the Luxembourg proceedings.

C A Kennedy Co v Stibbe-Monk Ltd (1976) 23 CBR (NS) 81

An Ontario Court recognised the private appointment of a receiver in England, on the grounds that a privately-appointed receiver had the same rights to the debtor's property as a court-appointed receiver.

Chapter 6

CAYMAN ISLANDS

1. Under general law

As a colony of the United Kingdom, the Cayman Islands' courts and legal system are very similar to those of the United Kingdom. Indeed the Grand Court Law 1975, section 20(2) (GCL) provides that the practice and procedure of the High Court of England will be applied in the Superior Grand Cayman Court where no contrary provision is made in local rules.

The insolvency court is the Grand Court which sits as the chief insolvency court (GCL, section 15).

At common law, a foreign judgment *in personam* is considered to create a "debt" between parties. The common law doctrine of obligation, and not comity, is the basis on which foreign judgments are recognised (the Grand Court case *Cause No 8 of 1988*, Cayman Islands Bulletin, No 2, September 1990).

A judgment of a foreign creditor may be enforced either:

– under common law rules; or
– if registered under the Foreign Judgments Reciprocal Enforcement Law (Revised) 1976, which gives the judgment the same force and effect as if it had originally been made in the Cayman Islands. The applicability of these laws to foreign insolvency proceedings is restricted to judgments made in the course of insolvency proceedings abroad that require the payment of money or are in relation to moveable property of the debtor.

2. Assisting legislation

The Cayman Islands' courts will accord recognition to a foreign bankruptcy relating to an individual under the Bankruptcy Law (Revised), section 156 which provides that all courts in bankruptcy shall act in aid of, and auxiliary to, each other on all matters of bankruptcy. Any order of one court in a proceeding in bankruptcy may, on application to another court, be made an order of such court and may be carried into effect accordingly.

A similar provision does not appear in the companies law that governs liquidations of companies although it is likely that the Grand Court will follow the Bankruptcy Law.

A foreign claimant may also apply for the bankruptcy of an individual or the winding-up of a company following the procedures set out under the Bankruptcy Law or the Company Law.

3. Insolvency practice

The Grand Court has taken a positive approach to recognising the status of an administrator appointed by a foreign court. It will recognise a foreign administrator appointed by a foreign court provided that the Grand Court is satisfied there is a sufficient connection between the defendant company and the jurisdiction in which the foreign administrator was appointed.

Foreign administrators not appointed by a relevant court, such as receivers and managers under a floating charge, may not receive the same recognition.

Foreign creditors have the right to prove their debts in the local insolvency proceedings of a natural or legal person and rank equally with local creditors. All provable debts rank equally.

As a leading offshore financial centre, the Cayman Islands has strict confidentiality laws which may cause problems for a foreign administrator seeking information about a Cayman Island debtor. The principal law is the Confidential Relationships (Preservation) Law 1976 (CRPL). Section 2 of the CRPL provides that confidential information will not be permitted to be disclosed except in the following circumstances:

- with the consent of the principal;
- in compliance with the direction of the Grand Court (section 3A); or
- pursuant to specific authorisation of the Governor.

However, it is accepted that the Grand Court may make orders for disclosure and enable the tracing of assets in certain circumstances. The onus is usually on the person holding the information to seek the directions of the court under the CRPL, section 3A.

4. Examples

Kilderkin Investments Limited (by its Receiver Manager) v *Player and six others* (1980–83)

A foreign receiver and manager appointed by the Superior Court of Ontario, Canada brought an action in the Cayman Islands to identify, preserve and recover assets of the defendant within the Cayman Islands. Assets were there as a result of alleged fraud or breach of trust.

The application for an order for the disclosure of assets was successful. The Grand Court ordered disclosure because a prima facie case of fraud and breach of trust had been established. Therefore it was the duty of the Court to assist the plaintiff to trace the assets. If information relating to the assets proved to be confidential and the principal's consent could not be obtained then an application would need to be made under the CRPL, section 3.

This case is also authority for the proposition that a foreign receiver may be recognised in the Cayman Islands provided that the court is satisfied that there is sufficient connection between the defendant company and the jurisdiction in which the receiver and manager was appointed.

In Re Be (1990–91 CILR Case Notes)

In this case Collett CJ held that the jurisdiction of the Cayman courts to recognise and assist a foreign receiver is derived from the obligations of comity to assist in the enforcement of the orders of a foreign court. No such obligations therefore arise in respect of a receiver who has been appointed under a debenture, since a Cayman court need not recognise his authority. The decision in *Kilderkin Investments* v *Player* was considered but not followed.

Chapter 7

COSTA RICA

1. Under general law

Nothing known.

2. Assisting legislation

None, in so far as we are aware: little information is available generally.

The Costa Rican Commercial Code of 30 April 1964, articles 851–967 govern the bankruptcy of companies and individuals in Costa Rica. The Civil Code applies to ownership of the debtor's property in Costa Rica and governs claims by foreign creditors to that property.

3. Insolvency practice

The existence of foreign insolvency proceedings will not affect Costa Rican creditors who may proceed to claim any assets located in Costa Rica. The Costa Rican branches or agencies of a foreign bankrupt (whether company, individual or partnership) may be placed into bankruptcy in Costa Rica at the request of a foreign administrator, who will be recognised in this limited way.

The Costa Rican branch of a foreign bankrupt may be declared bankrupt if it is unable to pay its debts. The order of priority for paying creditors is:

- local creditors who contracted directly with the branch;
- foreign creditors who contracted directly with the branch; and
- any surplus to the foreign debtor or foreign administrator.

4.   Examples

None available.

Chapter 8

DENMARK

1. Under general law

According to the Danish Bankruptcy Act (*Konkursloven*) No 588 of 1 September 1986, article 6, the Minister of Justice is entitled to issue guidelines under which foreign insolvency orders issued by foreign courts and authorities are recognisable and enforceable in Denmark provided they are not in breach of public policy. Apart from the Nordic Bankruptcy Convention of 7 November 1933, which includes the five Nordic countries (Denmark, Sweden, Norway, Finland and Iceland), the Minister of Justice has not used his authority to issue such guidelines.

Accordingly, a foreign insolvency order will, as a general rule, not be recognised in Denmark and does not prevent either proceedings against the debtor's assets in Denmark or an independent Danish insolvency being declared. The same applies to other foreign remedies, such as suspensions of payments and schemes of compositions. A foreign insolvency estate will only be entitled to take possession of the debtor's assets if insolvency could not have been adjudged in Denmark and a judgment to enable this to happen must first be obtained from a Danish court.

The Danish Bankruptcy Act (DBA) does not prevent a foreign creditor from filing a petition in bankruptcy against his Danish debtor. DBA, section 3 determines the competent court depending on the area of jurisdiction where the debtor performs his "economic activities" or his place of domicile. If the debtor does not have an established place of residence, the court having jurisdiction is that in the place where the debtor sojourns or the last place where he is known to have resided or sojourned. If Danish courts do not have jurisdiction according to DBA, section 3, the debtor cannot be declared insolvent in Denmark, even if the debtor has assets or property in Denmark.

Whether legal proceedings to recover assets belonging to the debtor in Denmark can be initiated depends on whether Danish courts have jurisdiction. For EU Member States, this issue is governed by the EC Convention on Enforcement of Judgments 1968 (EC Convention); for the Nordic countries it is governed by the Nordic Judgment Convention 1934 and for other countries by the Danish Act on Administration of Justice. As a general rule, Danish courts have jurisdiction if:

- the debtor is domiciled in Denmark;
- the debtor resides in Denmark without any established domicile;
- the debtor has left Denmark but has not yet established a domicile abroad;
- the debtor's principal place of business is in Denmark.

In addition, legal proceedings other than insolvency may be instituted if the debtor's assets or other property are located in Denmark.

A foreign creditor commencing legal proceedings in Denmark may have to provide security for costs made at the debtor's (defendant's) request.

Legal proceedings to seize the debtor's assets initiated in Denmark are governed by Danish private international law, which is based on the provisions of the EC Convention or—for non-EC Member States—Danish Act No 122 of 15 April 1964.

A judgment, other than an insolvency judgment ordered by a foreign court, may be recognised, in Denmark in accordance with the EC Convention or the Nordic Judgment Convention. Such judgments are directly enforceable in the bailiff's courts unless inconsistent with public policy. Other foreign court decisions are not recognised in Denmark but may—and often will—influence the Danish court's view upon a case.

2.   Assisting legislation

The only existing legislation is the Nordic Bankruptcy Convention of 1 September 1934 (Nordic Bankruptcy Convention) which has Denmark, Sweden, Norway, Finland and Iceland as contracting states. This Convention contains provisions with regard to bankruptcies declared in the Nordic countries.

The principal rule is that a bankruptcy declared in Denmark also includes the debtor's property in the other Nordic countries and vice versa. In other words, the Nordic Bankruptcy Convention provides for full recognition of bankruptcy decrees from all the Nordic countries without the need for an exequatur. The law applicable is the law of the country in which the insolvency proceedings were initiated, except for issues about the legal effect of the insolvency on the debtor's assets in other contracting states regarding securities, execution, etc.

The Nordic Bankruptcy Convention has given rise to few disputes. Case law is almost non-existent, which indicates that the Convention seems to be working in practice.

3. Insolvency practice

An insolvent estate includes all the debtor's property, including assets situate in foreign countries. The debtor is obliged to co-operate with the administrator by providing information to assist the recovery of assets, including foreign assets.

If an insolvent estate includes foreign assets, it is the administrator's duty to recover these assets. This problem is most often solved by the Danish authorities and courts providing the administrator with the necessary official certificates and documents confirming that the administrator has authority over the assets situate abroad.

A foreign creditor having a claim in a Danish estate will only have to notify his claim to the administrator who will determine whether the claim is acknowledged or not. Foreign creditors rank equally with the other creditors of the insolvent estate. If a foreign creditor has obtained a dividend through the debtor's insolvency in the creditor's own country, this dividend is regarded as a partial payment of the claim and only the remainder of the claim will be acknowledged by the administrator.

A foreign estate has legal capacity and legal personality in Denmark, meaning that the estate may be a party to litigation, but a foreign insolvency order does not affect the debtor's property in Denmark and a foreign administrator has no power to deal with the debtor's assets unless covered by the Nordic Bankruptcy Convention of 1 September 1934. Pending a court order, the debtor's property remains at his disposal. However, the foreign estate has the possibility of initiating any legal proceedings provided for in Danish law, including insolvency proceedings providing the Danish courts have jurisdiction.

If Danish private international law dictates that the law of a foreign country is applicable to the contractual relationship between the debtor and the foreign creditor, the law will apply to the contract notwithstanding the Danish insolvency proceedings. An exception to this is that Danish law for the protection of creditors will apply if the asset was situate in Denmark at the time of the issue of the decree.

Proceedings to set aside a transaction may be instituted if Danish courts have jurisdiction over the claim according to the Danish Act on Administration of Justice, *e.g.*, if the assets or the property affected by the claim are in Denmark. The EC Convention on Enforcement of Judgments 1968 does not apply in these cases.

4. Examples

There is little helpful case law: most of the cases seem to concern retention of title.

Chapter 9

EGYPT

1. Under general law

Egyptian courts will recognise and enforce a foreign judgment against an Egyptian debtor, or his property, if the state where the judgment was entered grants reciprocal treatment of Egyptian judgments. There are no treaties governing this; therefore it will be determined on the facts of the case.

The authorities are, however, inconsistent. One view is that any bankruptcy adjudication brought to Egypt for enforcement against an Egyptian debtor's property will be enforced in the same manner as any foreign judgment would be enforced in Egypt. An exequatur of the judgment must be obtained from an Egyptian court of first instance which will wish to establish that:

-   the foreign court had jurisdiction in the matter;
-   the debtor was properly served and properly represented in the proceedings;
-   there is no conflict with Egyptian public policy in enforcing the judgment;
-   there is no conflicting prior judgment in the same proceedings;
-   the judgment is final and enforceable; and
-   reciprocity exists.

The alternative view is that a foreign creditor must commence Egyptian bankruptcy proceedings.

2. Assisting legislation

There is no specific legislation to assist a foreign administrator to gain access to, or recognition by, an Egyptian court. The Code of Commerce 1883, section 368 provides that distribution of a debtor's assets will not be made until an amount has been set aside for foreign claims.

3.   Insolvency practice

Provided a foreign administrator can satisfy the Egyptian court as to his authority, he can participate in any local proceedings concerning the bankrupt and therefore would be recognised by the Egyptian court. Proof of authority is usually taken to include notarised documents from the appointing court as evidence that the foreign administrator was duly appointed. These documents must be legalised at an Egyptian consulate and translated into Arabic by a court translator.

Foreign creditors participate on an equal basis.

The court presumes no procedural irregularity in the foreign proceedings. A debtor with actual notice will be assumed to have had an opportunity to be represented. In general, Egyptian courts appear impartial in granting relief to foreign investors or lenders. Parties will bear their own costs unless there is a specific prior agreement that costs will be recoverable.

There is nothing to prohibit foreign creditors participating in Egyptian bankruptcies but they should act by appointing a local proxy.

4.   Examples

None known.

Chapter 10

ENGLAND AND WALES

1. Under general law

English case law shows a clear tradition of assistance and co-operation with foreign courts to enable foreign creditors to gain access to property situate in England and Wales. Foreign insolvency proceedings do not bar the commencement of English insolvency proceedings; the existence of such proceedings will be a factor to be considered in deciding whether concurrent proceedings should be commenced in England and Wales. The English courts will renounce jurisdiction if they consider that it is in the interest of justice and convenience that matters be administered solely in the foreign proceedings rather than in concurrent English proceedings.

The English court's attitude to recognition of foreign insolvency orders is selective although it is based principally upon unity and universality.

The English courts will have jurisdiction over an individual debtor if he:

- is either domiciled in England or Wales at the time of presentation of the petition;
- is personally present in England or Wales at the time of presentation of the petition; or
- habitually resided or carried on business in England or Wales in the three years prior to the date the petition is presented.

The fact that a foreign debtor may have assets in England and Wales is not a sufficient ground alone for the English courts to accept jurisdiction for the debtor's bankruptcy. Conversely, it has become established practice for the English courts to refuse to make a bankruptcy order if it can be shown that a foreign debtor has no assets within their jurisdiction.

Jurisdiction over a company is determined by considering whether the company has a sufficiently close connection with England and Wales. The definition of a company for the purposes of the Insolvency Act 1986 (the "Act") does not necessarily include a foreign incorporated company according to recent authority (*Re BCCI SA & Re BCCI (Overseas) Ltd* (1993) BCC 787 *and Devon & Somerset Farmers Limited* [1993] BCC 140). In *Re International Bulk commodities Ltd* [1992] BCC 463 the judges disagreed with this interpretation but recent decisions are in line with the former cases. The significance of this is that if a foreign incorporated company is not "a company" under the Act, it can only be wound up as an unregistered company.

2. Assisting legislation

English insolvency orders are deemed to have universal effect. All the property owned by a bankrupt individual, wherever situate, will vest in his trustee in bankruptcy according to the Act Section 306. A winding-up order also purports to have universal effect in that whilst a company's assets do not automatically vest in a liquidator, he has power to take possession and control of all the company's property wherever situate.

Section 426(1)–(3) of the Act provides for the mandatory reciprocal enforcement of orders made by a United Kingdom court exercising its insolvency jurisdiction between different parts of the United Kingdom including Scotland and Northern Ireland. However, there are certain limitations with regard to the enforcement of court orders against property in different parts of the United Kingdom in that, for example, an English administrator will only have such powers to act in relation to Scottish property as a Scottish administrator would have in his position.

Section 426(4) of the Act states as a general principle, that English courts with insolvency jurisdiction have an obligation to assist their counterparts in any other part of the United Kingdom and in any "prescribed jurisdiction".

Section 426(5) of the Act provides that in assisting their counterparts, English courts may apply the insolvency law of either jurisdiction on being requested to do so. English courts have a discretion as to the way in which the assistance will be given and must have regard to rules of private international law.

For the purposes of sections 426(4) and 426(5) of the Act, the countries prescribed by statutory instrument are as follows:

 – Anguilla;
 – Australia;
 – Bailiwick of Guernsey (including Alderney and Sark);
 – Bermuda;
 – Botswana;
 – Canada;
 – Cayman Islands;

-   Falkland Islands;
-   Gibraltar;
-   Hong Kong;
-   Malaysia;
-   Montserrat;
-   New Zealand;
-   Republic of Ireland;
-   Republic of South Africa;
-   St Helena;
-   The Bahamas
-   Turks and Caicos Islands;
-   Tuvalu; and
-   Virgin Islands;

The majority of these countries are either Commonwealth countries or have provisions comparable to section 426 of the Act.

3.   Insolvency practice

The procedure under section 426 of the Act is that the foreign administrator will petition his local court to issue a letter of request to the English courts for their assistance. The English courts have a discretion as to the assistance they will give but may only provide assistance in matters regulated by the Act.

There is recent authority for the English courts applying English law when requested to do so by the court of a prescribed country even where no equivalent provision existed under the foreign insolvency law. Conversely, whether the English courts could give effect to a foreign insolvency law provision which had no equivalent in English law is unclear, but it is thought that the courts would apply the provisions if it was not inconsistent with English insolvency law and public policy.

The English courts have a final discretion as to whether they will make an insolvency order and the presence of assets will be taken into account. The provisions as to corporate voluntary arrangements, administration orders and creditors' voluntary liquidations do not generally apply to foreign companies, although in *Re Dallhold Estates (UK) Pty Ltd* [1992] BCC 394, the English Court applied section 426 such that an administration order was made in respect of a foreign corporation.

Where the English courts have jurisdiction, the effect of insolvency proceedings commenced in England and Wales depends on the facts of the case. English proceedings may be limited to the administration of assets situated in England and Wales for the benefit of all creditors, foreign and English, or the proceedings may have universal effect. If the debtor's domicile is in the country where the foreign insolvency proceedings are initiated, it is unlikely that the

English courts will consider the English insolvency order to have a universal effect and English proceedings will be ancillary to the foreign proceedings. The English administrator will therefore remit funds to his foreign counterpart when English priority claims have been dealt with *(Re Commercial Bank of South Australia (1886)* 33 ChD 174).

In respect of an insolvent individual, if the relevant foreign law provides for a general assignment of a debtor's assets to his foreign administrator, the English courts will recognise the administrator's rights to any of the debtor's moveable property situate in England provided that the English courts do not have jurisdiction in respect of the debtor. In addition, the English courts will tend to recognise the jurisdiction of a foreign court provided the foreign insolvency order is extra-territorial in effect. Immoveable property will not vest in the foreign administrator automatically, but he may apply to the English courts requesting that they appoint him as receiver of the rents and profits of the property situate in England.

In respect of an insolvent company, the English courts will recognise a foreign insolvency order provided it is made in the company's country of domicile, although the vesting of the company's English assets in the foreign administrator as a result of the foreign insolvency order will not be recognised. A foreign administrator instead has the right to apply to the English courts for an order empowering him to recover and realise their English assets subject to any rights attaching to the assets before the application. In exercising their discretion to grant relief to the foreign administrator, the English courts will bear in mind the effect on English creditors, and if they would be prejudiced by being required to claim in the foreign insolvency, the English courts will not generally allow the assets to be handed over to the control of the foreign administrator. Ancillary insolvency proceedings may be commenced in England in these circumstances.

Foreign creditors claiming in English insolvency proceedings of any sort may lodge proofs of debt and participate in distributions. The English courts are keen to see that assets are shared equitably amongst all creditors and a creditor who is subject to the jurisdiction of the English courts, and who has already had the benefit of a foreign execution, may be required to surrender the fruits of his execution for the general benefit of all the creditors.

4. Examples

Re BCCI SA and Re BCCI (Overseas) Ltd **[1993] BCC 787**

A letter of request was issued by the Grand Court in the Cayman Islands for assistance under section 426(5) of the Insolvency Act (the Act) in making orders against the officers of BCCI (Overseas) Ltd, a Cayman Island company, which was being wound up in the Cayman Islands. The effect of the orders sought was anticipated to be the recovery of assets for the benefit of the liquidation. The letter of request asked the English courts to consider making orders against the officers under the following provisions of the Act:

- Section 212—Misfeasance in breach of fiduciary duty;
- Section 213—Fraudulent trading;
- Section 214—Wrongful trading; or
- Section 238—Transactions at an undervalue.

Rattee J held that the English courts had a discretion to apply the provisions of the Act notwithstanding the fact that there were no equivalent provisions under Cayman Islands' law. He took the view that if he refused to apply the provisions of the Act, it would defeat the purpose of section 426 since if the requesting court had corresponding powers under its local law, it would not need to request assistance from the English courts. He also indicated that the English courts should be predisposed to exercise their discretion in favour of giving assistance unless there was a very good reason for not providing assistance.

In addition, Rattee J indicated that the word "company" as used in the Act means only a United Kingdom incorporated company.

Re Dallhold Estates (UK) Pty Ltd [1992] BCC 394

Dallhold Estates (UK) Pty Ltd (Estates) was an Australian company which was a wholly-owned subsidiary of an English company. Estates went into liquidation in Australia and provisional liquidators were appointed in both Australia and England. The main asset of Estates was a lease of a property in England. The terms of that lease were such that if a winding-up order was made the landlord would be entitled to terminate the lease by re-entry and there was no entitlement to relief from forfeiture because the lease was an agricultural tenancy. It was therefore decided to place Estates into administration. An application under section 8 of the Insolvency Act 1986 for an administration order was not considered possible because Estates was a foreign-registered company and an application was therefore made under section 426 of the Act for an administration order.

Chadwick J granted the request of the Australian court for assistance in making an administration order. He interpreted the provisions of section 426 (4) of the Act strictly such that if the basic conditions for making an administration order were satisfied, the order must be made because the court was obliged to assist a foreign court under section 426(4).

Later cases have indicated that section 426(4) of the Act should not necessarily be interpreted in this way but rather that the court should always have an overriding discretion as to the relief that should be granted.

Chapter 11

FRANCE

1. Under general law

French insolvency law contains both principles of territoriality and universality which apply depending upon the circumstances of the case. If a French court has jurisdiction over an individual or a company, bankruptcy proceedings can usually be opened in France. If no other bankruptcy proceedings have been opened in respect of a debtor, the principle of universality is applicable and French bankruptcy law will apply to all the debtor's assets wherever situate. If there are multiple bankruptcies, then principles of territoriality are applicable unless France is a party to a treaty with the foreign requesting state.

A foreign administrator may gain access to the courts by using French civil law. The Civil Code, article 2123, provides that a foreign judgment including a bankruptcy order may be executed following the granting by a French court of an exequatur in respect of the assets of the debtor. This requires that:

- French courts must not have exclusive jurisdiction due to conflict of jurisdiction rules;
- the jurisdiction asserted by the applicant must be acceptable to French courts;
- the choice of foreign court must not be fraudulent;
- the foreign court must be competent to make the bankruptcy order; and
- the foreign judgment must not be fraudulent and must not contradict French public policy.

In granting the exequatur and determining the foreign administrator's powers, French courts may apply the law applicable to the foreign bankruptcy order. The Tribunal de Grande Instance issues the exequatur. It will not examine the merits of the foreign judgment but it will ensure that the five prerequisites are satisfied.

Access to the courts by a foreign administrator and recognition of his powers and foreign insolvency proceedings depends upon the jurisdiction of French courts to open French insolvency proceedings. French courts will have jurisdiction if either the debtor's legal seat is in France, or either the debtor or a creditor is a French citizen (Civil Code, articles 14 and 15). Recent case law indicates that if the debtor has taken part in trading activities in France, French courts will also have jurisdiction. The court of the debtor's main French establishment will be the competent court if the debtor does not have its legal seat in France.

2. Assisting legislation

There is no specific assisting legislation in French insolvency law which allows a foreign administrator to gain access to the French courts or which allows recognition of his powers or the foreign insolvency proceedings. Neither are there any provisions for opening ancillary insolvency proceedings following a foreign bankruptcy.

France is a party to bilateral treaties to facilitate access and recognition of foreign insolvency proceedings with Belgium, Italy, Monaco and Austria. These conventions provide jurisdiction to the courts of the state in which the debtor is domiciled (for a company, the place of its registered office). According to these treaties, a bankruptcy order will be recognised in the other contracting state, but an exequatur must be obtained to enforce it. The courts of the other treaty countries must refuse to open further bankruptcy proceedings once proceedings are commenced in the place of domicile.

3. Insolvency practice

The effect of a foreign bankruptcy order is limited unless a French court becomes involved. It will not prevent the debtor disposing of French assets or individual creditors attacking French assets. An administrator appointed by a foreign court may undertake certain acts in France in this capacity, including initiating proceedings or seeking provisional remedies. However, despite this limited recognition he has little power to act in France until he obtains an exequatur of the foreign bankruptcy order.

Once the foreign administrator has obtained an exequatur, he may commence execution proceedings in France, including attaching and selling French assets of the debtor. The granting of an exequatur to a foreign insolvency order generally prevents the opening of local proceedings. If French bankruptcy proceedings are commenced, attachments or other execution cannot proceed as all individual actions against the debtor are suspended under French law. Foreign creditors are entitled to claim in the French bankruptcy and they will be treated in the same manner as French creditors by the French courts.

If there are multiple bankruptcies including French proceedings, principles of strict territoriality will apply. The foreign bankruptcy will not affect French assets which are the exclusive domain of the French bankruptcy proceedings and will be restricted to French creditors.

4. Examples

In the *BCCI* proceedings, French insolvency proceedings were opened over the French branch of BCCI in spite of the existence of foreign insolvency proceedings.

Chapter 12

GERMANY

1. Under general law

Until a landmark decision of the German Federal Court of Justice on 11 July 1985, German insolvency proceedings were regarded as having universal effect whereas foreign insolvency proceedings were regarded as having only territorial effect. Therefore foreign insolvency orders were not recognised in Germany at all. The foreign administrator was recognised as the legal representative of the debtor, but his actions on the basis of the foreign insolvency order were not recognised in Germany.

While the decision of 11 July 1985 relates to the territory of the former West Germany only, general principles also apply in the territory of the former East Germany where they were codified in the Collective Enforcement Act (*Gesamtvoll-streckungsordnung* (CEA) 1991, section 22). In that case, the principle of universality was extended to foreign insolvency proceedings in that a foreign insolvency order was recognised subject to certain restrictions. Without any further formality, a foreign order will now have the same effect in Germany as under the law of the state in which the order was made. The effect of this is to enable a foreign administrator to take action in respect of assets situate in Germany.

The foreign insolvency order must comply with the following conditions:

- the order must have been made in accordance with the foreign law governing the bankruptcy;
- the foreign administrator must be authorised under the law governing the bankruptcy to administer and dispose of foreign assets; and
- under the law governing the bankruptcy the order must have effect on all the debtor's assets, wherever situate.

If the order fulfils the above conditions, it will be recognised in Germany in the following circumstances:

- the foreign proceedings must qualify as "bankruptcy proceedings" in accordance with German law. Generally, the proceedings must provide some form of collective procedure usually, but not exclusively, by way of liquidation and distribution of assets;
- the foreign insolvency court must have jurisdiction over the debtor under the rules of German international bankruptcy law. Jurisdiction will be recognised if the debtor's principal place of business, domicile, residence or the place where the debtor has an establishment or manages a property as owner, user or lessee is in the foreign state; and
- recognition of the foreign insolvency order does not contradict German principles of public policy.

There are separate rules as to the recognition of other orders made by foreign courts in the course of insolvency proceedings as opposed to the order by which foreign insolvency proceedings are commenced. These orders are subject to the general rules on the recognition and enforcement of foreign judgments as set out at sections 328 and 722/723 of the German Code of Civil Procedure (CCP) which is applicable to the entire German territory.

The CCP provisions allow the enforcement of orders which assist the foreign administrator in the performance of his functions, including orders requiring information, requiring the debtor to co-operate, redirecting the debtor's mail and relating to the determination of disputed claims. If these orders are final and binding under the law of the state in which they were rendered, the foreign administrator may seek to have them declared enforceable in Germany provided:

- the foreign court had jurisdiction to make the order under the principles of German law;
- the debtor was properly notified of the commencement of the proceedings and was given an opportunity to be represented;
- the order is not incompatible with a previous decision of a German court or a foreign court which is recognised in Germany, and the foreign proceedings are not incompatible with proceedings which are already pending in Germany;
- the recognition of the order is consistent with basic principles of German law; and
- there is reciprocity.

2. Assisting legislation

In Germany, there is no express assisting legislation at present.

The current rules on international insolvency and access to the courts will be superseded as from 1 January 1999 when the Introductory Act to the Insolvency

Act (the Act) will enter into force in Germany. The Act will apply to Germany as a whole but will not be as wide ranging as had been hoped. Initially, it was intended to adopt comprehensive provisions similar in substance to those set out in the draft European Union Bankruptcy Convention. However, the German Parliament has adopted instead a limited codification on the basis of the existing case law principles and the Collective Enforcement Act 1991 section 22. Article 102 of the Act will provide for the recognition of foreign insolvency proceedings including access to the debtor's assets situate in Germany.

Article 102 will include special conflict rules governing setting aside antecedent transactions. Currently the issue of the applicable law to such actions is disputed under German international insolvency law. However, under the new rule if the transaction is detrimental to creditors, then the primary law to be applied will be the foreign insolvency law, provided German law, which governs the effects of the transaction to be set aside, is taken into account to protect the German public.

Under article 102, German insolvency proceedings comprising only a foreign debtor's assets situate in Germany may be commenced if the debtor has any assets in Germany. This is not possible under existing provisions which provide that a debtor, who does not have his principal place of business or domicile or residence in Germany, must have an establishment or manage a property as owner, user or lessee in Germany before such an order can be made.

3. Insolvency practice

The recognition of foreign bankruptcy orders in Germany is limited at present.

If the German courts have jurisdiction over a debtor, German insolvency proceedings may be commenced and will have priority over the foreign proceedings. There is no provision for ancillary proceedings in Germany; once German insolvency proceedings are commenced in theory all assets are included in the German estate. The foreign administrator cannot commence German insolvency proceedings: a creditor (either foreign or German) must commence proceedings although there is no need to prove insolvency of the debtor where foreign bankruptcy proceedings exist. There are similar provisions set out in the Collective Enforcement Act (CEA) 1991, section 22 in respect of the former East German territory.

The German Bankruptcy Act (*Konkursordnung*) 1887, section 237, allows individual creditors to take execution measures against German assets of the debtor on the basis of pre-existing judgments despite the recognition of the foreign insolvency order. These provisions do not apply to the former East German territory where execution measures are not permitted once the foreign bankruptcy proceedings have been recognised. Under Article 102 of the Introductory Act to the Insolvency Act execution measures will no longer be permitted anywhere in Germany once the foreign insolvency proceedings have been recognised.

4. Examples

The Federal Court of Justice decision of 27 May 1993

A debtor who had been subject to bankruptcy proceedings in Switzerland was sued in Germany by a creditor to whom a loss certificate had been issued in Swiss bankruptcy proceedings. Under Swiss law loss certificates are issued to every creditor in respect of the part of the claim not satisfied in the Swiss bankruptcy proceedings. This is intended to restrict the creditors' rights of execution against the debtor in respect of the assets in the bankruptcy.

The German court recognised the effect of those certificates and stated that Swiss bankruptcy proceedings qualified as bankruptcy proceedings under German law standards. The Swiss courts were declared to have jurisdiction for the opening of bankruptcy proceedings under the rules of German international bankruptcy law. The courts held that the recognition of the effects of loss certificates issued in Swiss bankruptcy proceedings was not contrary to German principles of public policy.

Chapter 13

GIBRALTAR

1. Under general law

Gibraltar has its own reciprocal enforcement legislation which provides for the registration of judgments given in the superior courts of other countries.

The following countries are designated for the purposes of this legislation:

- Australia;
- Bermuda (The Bermudas or Somers Islands);
- Malta;
- Nigeria; and
- United Kingdom.

When a judgment has been registered in Gibraltar, it will have the same force and effect as if it had been made originally in the Supreme Court of Gibraltar.

The Judgments (European Community) (Enforcement) Ordinance provides that any decision, judgment or order enforceable under the European Economic Community Treaty, Articles 187 or 192, the Euratom Treaty, Articles 18, 159, or 164 or the European Coal and Steel Community Treaty, Articles 44 or 92, shall be registered at the Supreme Court of Gibraltar upon a duly-made application.

English common law applies in Gibraltar and therefore Gibraltarian courts have inherent jurisdiction to act in aid of, and be auxiliary to, every court in the United Kingdom or in any British possession having bankruptcy or insolvency jurisdiction.

2. Assisting legislation

The Gibraltar Bankruptcy Ordinance, section 98A, provides that the Gibraltarian courts will act in aid of and be auxiliary to United Kingdom courts in individual insolvency matters. There is, however, no express provision that the Supreme Court of Gibraltar will act in aid of a court in any other country in this respect. There is no corresponding provision for companies.

However, Gibraltar is a relevant country for the purpose of the United Kingdom Insolvency Act 1986, section 426 (4), (5) and (11) pursuant to the provisions of the Co-operation of Insolvency Courts (Designation of Relevant Countries and Territories) Order 1986 (SI 1986 No 2123). Therefore in corporate insolvency cases, the Supreme Court of Gibraltar may request the assistance of the United Kingdom courts, although it appears that the United Kingdom courts cannot request the assistance of the Supreme Courts of Gibraltar, as in individual insolvency cases.

3. Insolvency practice

Apart from the provisions above, no framework exists for the enforcement of foreign insolvency proceedings and, as such, there are no procedural steps to be followed.

In other insolvency matters, English insolvency practice is applied and English case law tends to be followed.

4. Examples

None available.

Chapter 14

GREECE

1. Under general law

Principles of unity and universality are important. According to the Greek constitution, article 20 paragraph 1, the Greek courts are generally accessible by any person, whether a foreigner or Greek. The Greek Civil Code, article 4, underlines this principle of equality for any claimant. Therefore the Greek courts will tend to recognise foreign claims whether by a foreign administrator or otherwise and grant assistance provided that the Greek courts have jurisdiction. The criteria under the Civil Procedure Code (CPC) to determine jurisdiction include:

– domicile or residence of the debtor including the legal seat or principal place of business of a company;
– the whereabouts of any immoveable property in dispute; and
– the place where a contract was concluded.

Once the jurisdiction of the Greek courts is established, their decisions are automatically assumed to have international effect.

2. Assisting legislation

No special procedure is required for the recognition of a foreign bankruptcy judgment under the Civil Procedure Code (CPC), article 780 and no pre-conditions need to be satisfied. However, an order or judgment which is not a bankruptcy judgment but is given in, or as a result of, bankruptcy proceedings, such as an order seeking information, may only be recognised as enforceable by a Greek court if the requirements of the CPC, articles 323 and 905 are met, including:

- the foreign order must not be contrary to public policy or Greek morality;
- the defendant must have had an opportunity to defend himself; and
- there must be no conflict with any judgment of the Greek courts.

There are no special requirements for a foreign claimant to give security before using a Greek court other than those applicable under general Greek civil law.

Bilateral treaties may assist in some matters, although it is not known whether these are still considered as applying to bankruptcy judgments or orders. Some of these treaties are effectively redundant due to political changes. The known treaties are:

Bulgaria 1978	Poland 1981
Cyprus 1985	Romania 1974
Czechoslovakia 1983	Syria 1984
Hungary 1981	USSR 1982
Lebanon 1980	Yugoslavia 1959

3. Insolvency practice

Foreign bankruptcy judgments are recognised in Greece and foreign administrators are entitled to take possession of moveable and immoveable Greek assets.

Greek law assumes that the bankruptcy of a Greek debtor, where his undertaking and most of his assets are domiciled in Greece under Greek law, will be recognised abroad and that a Greek administrator will be entitled to take possession of any assets abroad whether moveable or moveable.

4. Examples

Judgment 1111–1989 in the Piraeus Court of Appeal

A British bankruptcy order is valid in Greece pursuant to the Civil Procedure Code, article 780 and any further procedure is unnecessary.

Chapter 15

HONG KONG

1. Under general law

Hong Kong is currently a territory subject to British administration. Consequently, Hong Kong insolvency law as set out in the Companies Ordinance is
broadly modelled on the 1948 Companies Act and is influenced by United
Kingdom common law.

   English conflicts of law rules generally apply. A Hong Kong court has a discretion whether or not to provide assistance under its inherent jurisdiction. In
exercising that discretion, the Hong Kong court, presumably taking account of
factors similar to those considered by English courts, will either:

-   declare the debtor bankrupt or wind it up providing it has jurisdiction to
    do so; or
-   if it has no jurisdiction, or considers the interests of justice and con-
    venience require the debtor's assets to be administered in a single set of
    proceedings, recognise the effect of the foreign insolvency order and the
    rights of the foreign administrator to the assets.

2. Assisting legislation

There is no statutory requirement for the Hong Kong courts to co-operate with
foreign courts or foreign administrators.

3. Insolvency practice

There is no established trend in Hong Kong in favour of judicial co-operation
although recent case law is more favourable.

The procedure to be adopted to attempt to gain judicial co-operation is for the foreign bankruptcy court to issue a letter of request for assistance to the Hong Kong court who will consider whether to grant such assistance under its inherent jurisdiction.

In the case of a foreign bankruptcy of an individual wherein the bankruptcy order operates to transfer property to the trustee in bankruptcy and the bankruptcy order has international effect, the Hong Kong courts will recognise the transfer. This principle does not apply to real property, although the foreign administrator may apply to the Hong Kong courts for the appointment of a receiver of the real property in Hong Kong.

In the case of the winding-up of a foreign company, a liquidator appointed in the company's place of incorporation under an order purporting to have universal effect may act on behalf of the company in Hong Kong. The debtor's assets will not vest in the liquidator but his rights to recover and realise Hong Kong assets will be recognised. Where the foreign liquidator is appointed in a jurisdiction other than the place of incorporation, the position is not clear.

Foreign creditors' claims will be treated rateably with those of Hong Kong creditors. Foreign creditors commencing legal proceedings in Hong Kong may be required to provide security for costs.

4. Examples

In Re Aw Hoe (1957) Hong Kong Law Reports 409 & 539

The High Court of Singapore made an order for a letter of request to be issued to the Supreme Court of Hong Kong to act in aid of, and be auxiliary to, the Singapore Court for the purpose of realising the assets of the deceased debtor's estate in Hong Kong.

Gould J made an order whereby the property of the deceased situate in Hong Kong was vested in the Official Assignee in Singapore. The Official Assignee was also authorised to realise the property in Hong Kong and administer the same for the benefit of the creditors.

Mobil Sales & Supply Corporation v The Owners Of The Vessel "Pacific Bear" (1979) Hong Kong Law Reports 125

The defendant was an American company, incorporated in the United States and owning four ships. It ran into financial difficulties and filed for protection under Chapter 11 of the United States Bankruptcy Code with the District Court in North Carolina. As a result an automatic stay of proceedings against the debtor throughout the United States was imposed and the company was allowed to continue trading as a "debtor in possession". The plaintiff creditor, with other creditors, commenced proceedings in Hong Kong against the defendant and issued a writ *in rem* against some of its vessels. The defendant sought to set aside the writs and all subsequent proceedings on the grounds, *inter alia,* of the moratorium in the American Bankruptcy.

Cons J, accepted that the case of *Galbraith* v *Grimshaw* was authority for the general principle that where a court finds there is a process of universal distribution of a bankrupt's effects already pending, it should not allow steps to be taken in its territory which would interfere with the process of universal distribution.

However, the judge took the view that the rule in *Galbraith* had no application in this case because the defendant had not yet been made bankrupt.

Modern Terminals Ltd v States Steamship Company (1979) HKLR 512

Trainer J disagreed with the opinion expressed by Cons J above and applied the principle enunciated in *Galbraith* in this case where the facts were similar:

"... [a] debtor in possession is not the beneficial owner of the assets but holds them in trust for the benefit of the creditors with the right to have the title as beneficial owner revested in it if the terms of the arrangement with the creditors are fulfilled. It is true that a debtor in possession is still interested in the business and assets of the company but only in so far as they may one day be revested in it. In the instant case all the assets are being realised for the benefit of the creditors."

Re Irish Shipping Limited (1985) HKLR 436

In this case a winding-up order had already been made in Ireland in respect of a shipping company incorporated in that country. However, the Irish official liquidator petitioned for the winding-up of the company in Hong Kong on the grounds that the company was unable to pay its debts and it was just and equitable that an order be made notwithstanding that an order had already been made by the Irish High Court. The Irish liquidator wanted the winding-up order to be made in Hong Kong to enable him to take possession of and sell a ship which was situate in Hong Kong. Furthermore, the effect of the winding-up order in Hong Kong would stay other legal proceedings against the company including actions by opposing creditors who had instituted proceedings *in rem* against the vessel. If those proceedings were successful, the plaintiff creditors would be paid out of the sale proceeds in priority to other creditors.

The High Court of Hong Kong made the winding-up order on the Irish liquidator's petition. The Court took account of the interests of the unsecured creditors and the desirability that the Hong Kong courts should assist liquidators appointed by courts in other jurisdictions. The High Court also noted that the creditors opposing the petition wished to obtain an unfair advantage over the general body of creditors.

Chapter 16

INDIA

1. Under general law

Indian Courts have a well-developed approach consistent with accepted principles of private international law.

The recognition and enforcement of foreign judgments are governed by the India Civil Procedure Code 1908 (CPC), sections 13, 14 and 44A. The rules laid down by these sections are rules of substantive law and not mere procedural law *(Moloji Nar Rao* v *Shankar Saran,* AIR 1962, SC 1737 at 1741). The Code distinguished foreign judgments of countries declared by the Indian Government as reciprocating countries from judgments of those which are not.

Section 13 provides that a foreign judgment shall be conclusive as to any matter directly adjudicated upon between the same parties, or between parties through whom they claim litigating under the same title, provided the judgment:

- has been pronounced by a court of competent jurisdiction;
- has been given on the merits of the case;
- appears on the face of the proceedings to be founded on a correct view of international law and the law of India in cases in which such law is applicable;
- complies with natural justice and was not obtained by fraud; and
- sustains a claim which is not a breach of any law in force in India.

There is a presumption that these conditions have been satisfied. Therefore an Indian court will not inquire into the merits of the original claim or check if the conclusions are correct or supported by evidence. A domestic court will re-examine the foreign judgment only if it is challenged on the basis that one or more of the pre-conditions mentioned above is not satisfied.

Under the CPC, section 14, an Indian court shall presume upon the production of a duly authenticated copy of the foreign judgment that the foreign court had competent jurisdiction. The presumption may be rebutted by the defendant.

If a foreign judgment is given in a country which is not considered to be a reciprocating territory, the judgment debtor would have to file a suit based on the foreign judgment in an Indian court to have it recognised and enforced in India. An Indian court would grant the required order by following principles of comity provided the foreign judgment fulfils the pre-conditions set out in section 13.

In *Re Viswanathan and others* v *Rakn-ul-Malk Syed Abdul Wajid* (AIR 1963 S.C. 1), the Supreme Court made three observations with regard to the exercise of a court's jurisdiction when foreign judgments are sought to be enforced. An Indian court may recognise or enforce judgments *in rem*, if the subject matter of the action is within the foreign country. The Supreme Court will not deal directly or indirectly with judgments relating to the title to immoveable property situated outside the jurisdiction of the foreign court. Finally, the Court will not assist in the enforcement of foreign judgments in respect of penal or revenue laws.

Where a certified copy of a decree of a superior court of a foreign country considered to be a reciprocating territory has been filed in a District Court, the decree may be executed in India as if it was a judgment of an Indian court, the CPC (section 44A).

2. Assisting legislation

The Presidency Towns Insolvency Act 1909 (PTIA) and the Provincial Insolvency Act 1920 (PIA) apply to natural persons only: the Companies Act 1956 governs the winding-up of companies.

The PTIA, section 126, states that all courts having jurisdiction under this Act shall make such orders and do such things as may be necessary to give effect to the Bankruptcy Act 1883, section 118 and to the Provincial Insolvency Act 1907 (1907 Act), section 50.

The PIA, section 77, reproduces section 50 of the 1907 Act which states that all courts having jurisdiction in insolvency and the officers of such courts shall act severally in aid of, and be auxiliary to, each other in all matters of insolvency. Where a foreign court requests aid from an Indian court in enforcing its order, the Indian court may exercise such jurisdiction as either of the courts could exercise in similar matters within their respective jurisdictions.

There does not appear to be a similar provision in the Companies Act 1956.

3. Insolvency practice

Little is known.

4. Examples

N.A. Aiyaswamy Chetty v The Official Assignee of Madras — ILR Madras, vol 57, 1934, 616

On 9 January 1931, a person was adjudicated as insolvent in Penang, in the Straits Settlements (now Malaysia). On 15 March 1931 the applicant, an unsecured creditor, filed an action against the insolvent in Ramnad, part of the former British India. On 28 November 1931, the creditor obtained a decree and applied to execute the decree by the sale of the attached property.

In Penang the bankrupt executed a conveyance of Indian property, including the property under attachment, in favour of the Official Assignee in Bankruptcy of Penang. At the request of the Supreme Court of Penang, an order was made by the Madras High Court directing the Official Assignee of Madras to act auxiliary to the Official Assignee of Penang and take possession of the properties of the insolvent and realise the same. The Official Assignee in Madras applied to the Insolvency Court for an order staying the execution proceedings by the holder of the attaching decree. The order for a stay of execution was granted. The decree holder appealed.

Dismissing the appeal, the Court held that the execution proceedings were properly stayed since the attachment was later than the date of the adjudication of bankruptcy in Penang. The reasons given by Beasley CJ were:

"Stone J has based the order appealed against on another ground, namely, that this Court is acting in aid of and auxiliary to the Penang Court and that, since it is clearly the duty of a court within the Empire to aid other jurisdictions as effectively as possible, this Court will deem, pursuant to the rules of private international law, there to have been a vesting. In other words, this Court will deem the insolvent's immoveable property here to have vested in the Official Assignee of Penang on the date of the adjudication just as other immoveable property of the insolvent in the Straits Settlements would have done. If this Court is entitled to deem such a vesting, then clearly the appellant's attachment of the insolvent's immoveable property was after the date of the vesting and is ineffective."

Therefore, the test is whether, at the date of adjudication, the insolvent was free to dispose of the property, or whether there was anything which affected his power of disposal over the property.

Chapter 17

INDONESIA

1. Under general law

In Indonesia principles of territoriality apply. Therefore a judgment of a foreign court will not be enforced by an Indonesian court on the grounds that a judgment given in a foreign country cannot have a direct force of its own in another.

The Central Rules, section 22a, provides that the competence of a local court and the execution of its judgments are "limited by the principles recognised by the laws of nations". Thus, based upon the principle of territoriality, a court's decision may be enforced only within the state in which it has jurisdiction.

The Regulations on Civil Procedures, section 436, provides that foreign judgments cannot be enforced in the territory of Indonesia although there are exceptions in the Commercial Code, section 724, and other legislative instruments which are not relevant to this report. Although section 436 is no longer in force, the Indonesian courts use it as a guideline when considering an application to enforce a foreign judgment.

2. Assisting legislation

Indonesian statutes are silent on this issue.

3. Insolvency practice

The law relating to the recognition of a foreign order of a declaratory or constitutive nature is markedly different. The Indonesian courts will recognise and respect such orders because declaratory and constitutive judgments merely require recognition and not enforcement. Therefore, foreign insolvency orders may be recognised in Indonesia.

A foreign administrator may be recognised by an Indonesian court. It has been reported that the courts have recognised a foreign administrator as representing a bankrupt and allowed him to take possession of the bankrupt's estate.

A foreign creditor can, directly or through an assignee, prove a claim in a local bankruptcy.

4. Examples

None known.

Chapter 18

IRELAND

1. Under general law

A foreign administrator may obtain access to the Irish courts only by utilising rules of private international law as applied in Ireland. Legal action can be brought if the defendant is present, temporarily or otherwise, within the Irish jurisdiction.

A foreign administrator or creditor may either commence proceedings in the Irish courts or seek to have a judgment recognised in the jurisdiction. Whilst a foreign judgment will be recognised, it will not be directly enforced in Ireland. Therefore, the foreign administrator must institute fresh proceedings in the Irish courts by suing on the judgment obtained or bring fresh proceedings based on the original claim.

If an action is commenced, the Irish courts will have jurisdiction provided that the originating summons is duly served in accordance with the procedural rules as to issue and service. There is no distinction between an Irish and a foreign plaintiff. However, the Irish courts will not deal with actions involving foreign revenue law or foreign penal law. In addition a foreign plaintiff may be required to give security for costs.

Once jurisdiction and *locus standi* are established all remedies will be available to the foreign administrator including judgment orders, executions orders, examination orders, garnishee orders, and *Mareva* injunctions.

2. Assisting legislation

There are separate laws relating to individuals and companies.

Individuals

The Bankruptcy Act 1988 (1988 Act), section 142 gives the court and its officers an extensive, though discretionary, power to act in aid of courts of the following countries and their officers:

- Channel Islands;
- England & Wales;
- Isle of Man;
- Northern Ireland; and
- Scotland.

Section 142(2)(a) empowers the Government to extend the aid provisions to courts of other jurisdictions where it is satisfied that reciprocal facilities will be afforded in the other jurisdictions. There is little authority as to whether reciprocal facilities means broadly equivalent assistance or identical assistance to that afforded by the Irish courts under section 142(1). The courts have a discretion pursuant to section 142(1) as to what (if any) assistance will be given; it is not a mandatary section. Although there are no guidelines, the court will probably take into account procedural fairness, public policy, private international law rules and the existence of any conflicting bankruptcy. Aid will be refused if:

- the Irish court takes the view that the foreign bankruptcy court had no jurisdiction to make the debtor bankrupt; or
- the proceedings in the foreign court contravene natural justice; or
- the effect of granting aid would be to enforce the claims of a foreign revenue authority; this contravenes public policy.

An Irish court may appoint the foreign administrator as receiver with power to sell assets and distribute the proceeds to creditors while bearing in mind the claims of Irish creditors. Any dispute will be determined in the Irish courts.

Companies

The Companies Act 1963 (1963 Act), section 250 relating to orders made in winding-up by foreign courts and the Companies (Amendment) Act 1990 (1990 Act), section 36 relating to reconstruction orders made by foreign courts are virtually the same, and provide that winding-up or reconstruction orders by a court of a recognised country may be enforced by the Irish courts, as if the order had been made by the Irish courts. Only the United Kingdom is a recognised country with regard to section 250 and no countries have been recognised at all in respect of section 36. It is thought that the Irish courts may, under these sections, enforce orders which an Irish court itself has no original jurisdiction to make. However, the Irish courts have a general discretion which they are likely to use to avoid this.

No special procedures are laid down for the use of any of these sections, so the foreign administrator must utilise ordinary Irish civil proceedings.

3. Insolvency practice

The Irish courts are receptive to applications by foreign administrators but such applications are not common. It appears that there is a distinction between moveable and immoveable property with regard to the effect of foreign jurisdictions. Moveable property will be deemed to have vested in the foreign administrator where the relevant foreign law provides for such vesting. Land or interests in land do not generally vest in the foreign administrator although an Irish court may permit the foreign administrator to dispose of immoveable property for the benefit of the debtor's estate.

4. Examples

- *Buchanan* v *McVey* (1955) AC 516; and
- *Banco Ambrosiano* (1987) ILRM 669.

Chapter 19

ISRAEL

1. Under general law

The law governing recognition by the Israeli courts of a foreign bankruptcy is not settled. The Israeli courts rely on their own Supreme Court decisions and English common law to resolve aspects of Israeli law which require clarification. The latter is persuasive only and recently the Israeli courts have also looked to United States law for guidance. The Israeli courts will consider any agreement between the parties as to the applicable law.

The Foreign Judgment Enforcement Law 1958 (FJEL), section 11, gives the Israeli courts discretion to recognise a foreign judgment by a declaratory judgment provided:

- Israel must have specifically agreed to recognise foreign judgments of that kind with the foreign state in question and the judgment must fulfil the conditions of that agreement; and
- the judgment must be capable of enforcement under Israeli law.

A debtor can attempt to defeat the recognition or enforcement of a foreign judgment if:

- it was obtained by fraud; or
- the Israeli court does not recognise the jurisdiction of the foreign court, which jurisdiction is presumed if the debtor was resident or temporarily present in the foreign state when served with process; or
- proceedings are either pending or have been determined in an Israeli court; or
- the debtor was denied a reasonable opportunity to participate in the foreign proceedings in which the judgment was given.

In determining the competency of a foreign court to make a bankruptcy order an Israeli court would also consider:

- the locations of the debtor's principal place of business and assets; and
- whether the debtor submitted to the foreign jurisdiction.

If a foreign judgment is recognised it will be considered valid but cannot necessarily be executed.

In addition to its recognition, the FJEL, section 3, provides that the Israeli court may declare a foreign judgment to be enforceable if the following conditions are satisfied:

- the foreign court was competent to give judgment;
- the judgment is a final judgment; no appeal may be lodged;
- the obligation imposed by the judgment is enforceable under Israeli law;
- the judgment is not contrary to Israeli public policy; and
- the judgment is enforceable in the country in which it was given.

The FJEL, section 4, provides that there will be no enforcement unless an Israeli judgment could be enforced in the state where judgment was given. While Israeli courts look for reciprocity, they have a discretion to grant an order permitting enforcement if the Attorney-General makes the application. If a foreign judgment is enforced it shall have the effect of an Israeli judgment (section 10a). It may then be executed. The procedure for enforcement is set out in the Civil Procedure Regulations 1984, regulations 352–359.

2. Assisting legislation

There is no specific legislation dealing with recognition of a foreign administrator or foreign insolvency proceedings although recent authority suggests that the Israeli courts will follow general civil law. Therefore a court would look to the criteria for the recognition and enforcement of foreign civil orders and judgments.

Bilateral conventions to which Israel is a party include:

- Israel and Austria Convention for the reciprocal recognition and enforcement of judicial decisions in civil and commercial matters, 6 June 1966;
- Israel, the United Kingdom and Northern Ireland Convention on the reciprocal recognition and enforcement of judicial decisions in civil matters, 28 October 1970; and
- Israel and Germany Convention for the reciprocal recognition and enforcement of court decisions in civil and commercial matters, 20 July 1977.

It is not known whether any of these conventions have been applied by the courts to foreign insolvency orders or orders made in the course of foreign insolvency proceedings.

3. Insolvency practice

Because of the influence of English common law and United States bankruptcy law, the Israeli courts will tend to exercise their discretion in deciding whether to grant access and recognition to a foreign administrator. If a foreign administrator is recognised by the Israeli courts he will be entitled to moveable property but not usually immoveable property. Reciprocity is an important factor to Israeli courts.

Israeli bankruptcy law embraces universality. If a judgment or order of the Israeli courts is not recognised in a foreign jurisdiction where assets are located, the debtor can be obliged to grant a power of attorney to the Israeli administrator to enable him to deal with the foreign property.

Foreign creditors are entitled to participate in Israeli insolvency proceedings on the basis of an equal distribution. No special requirements attach to foreign creditors' claims. A foreign creditor participating in Israeli insolvency proceedings is subject to the jurisdiction of the Israeli courts in any counterclaim by the debtor. "Hotchpotch" rules will apply.

4. Examples

Dayan v EDS International Limited (II) 38 P 99 (1984)

The Israeli Supreme Court recognised a court order made in Canadian insolvency proceedings requiring a company to deliver up to the Canadian administrator goods transferred from Canada to Israel.

The provisions of the FJEL, section 11(b), were applied. The Court indicated there that the standards for determining whether a foreign judgment should be recognised are no stricter than the standards used by Israeli courts in deciding whether to enforce a foreign judgment. The Canadian administrator had the right to possession of the goods because the title had been conferred on him by order of the Canadian bankruptcy courts.

CA490/88 Dr Anba Ahmad et al 44 (iv) (1990) at 397–405

The Israeli Supreme Court referred to the decision in the *Dayan* case and adopted Vice President Ben-Porat's ruling in that case regarding the FJEL, section 11(b).

Chapter 20

ITALY

1. Under general law

The recognition and enforcement of foreign judgments (including foreign insolvency orders) is provided for in the Civil Procedure Code 1942 (CPC). The procedure for obtaining recognition of foreign judgments is set out in the CPC, articles 796 and 797. A petition must be filed with the Corte d'Appelo of the place where the foreign administrator wishes the adjudication of insolvency to be enforced. Article 797 requires that:

- the foreign adjudication must be final and conclusive;
- it must not be contrary to Italian public policy and there should not be significant differences between the Italian bankruptcy procedure and the foreign bankruptcy procedure; and
- there must be no conflicting litigation pending in the Italian courts and no conflict with any Italian judgment.

Articles 802 and 803 of the CPC enable the execution of a foreign judgment so recognised.

2. Assisting legislation

The Italian Insolvency Proceedings Act No 267 1942 (Bankruptcy Act) does not refer to foreign insolvency proceedings. A foreign administrator must use the general civil procedure set out above. Filing a request to give effect to a foreign insolvency order prevents the Italian courts hearing a domestic insolvency petition.

Bankruptcy proceedings are required by Italian law if an entrepreneur debtor (company, partnership or individual) is unable to pay matured debts. Public bodies, agricultural entrepreneurs and small traders cannot be made bankrupt in Italy.

The Bankruptcy Act 1942, section 9, and the Civil Procedure Code 1942, article 4, set out rules on jurisdiction over foreigners and provide that Italian insolvency proceedings may be commenced in respect of a non-resident debtor if:

- the debtor is in default of obligations undertaken or to be performed in Italy, although some courts also require the debtor to have assets in Italy for the benefit of Italian creditors; and
- the debtor is engaged in business in Italy with either the main location or a permanent branch or office in Italy.

If a foreign insolvency order is not recognised under the above procedure, separate insolvency proceedings may be initiated under the Bankruptcy Act, section 9 by a petition filed by either a creditor, the public prosecutor or the debtor.

Section 9 also appears to envisage international treaties being concluded, although the only known treaties with insolvency implications are:

- The Rome Treaties between France and Italy—30 June 1930
  These provide that:

  - bankruptcy orders in either country will be final judgments in the other state provided enabling judgments are obtained before enforcement;
  - jurisdiction is determined by the situation of the debtor's principal business address (individual) or legal address (partnership/company);
  - claims concerning immoveable property must be processed in the courts of the country where the property is located;
  - the law of the country where the bankruptcy was adjudicated governs:

    - the appointment of an administrator and his powers; and
    - determination of claims.

- The Convention between the Republic of San Marino and Italy of 31 November 1939;
- The Rome Treaties between the United Kingdom and Italy—7 February 1964
  In the limited context of insolvency these Treaties must be deemed to be still in force although the countries have since ratified the 1968 Brussels Convention. They are not of great assistance since the only relevant provision states that jurisdiction is determined by reference to the procedural rules of the country where enforcement is sought; and
- The Rome Treaty between Austria and Italy of 12 July 1977.

3. Insolvency practice

Unless a treaty exists, the foreign administrator must:

- use the Civil Procedure Code (CPC) procedure and seek the registration of the foreign insolvency in Italy; and
- petition for a secondary insolvency in Italy provided the relevant conditions are satisfied.

It may take some time to obtain an exequatur under the CPC, article 797, and the assets may be dispersed by the debtor during that time. Prior to obtaining the exequatur, therefore, a foreign administrator should consider obtaining an attachment of the local assets. He can only recover assets in the possession of the debtor. He cannot recover assets from bona fide third parties although he may apply for revocation of payments to creditors before the insolvency order. The exequatur will not prevent secured creditors or creditors who have taken enforcement proceedings from recovering assets.

The object of the execution of the foreign insolvency adjudication (once registered) must be located in Italy. The foreign administrator should realise the assets and distribute sums due to creditors who have claimed in the foreign insolvency. Any amount remaining will be distributed to creditors who have failed to prove their claims in accordance with the foreign insolvency requirements and any disputes will be resolved by an Italian judge. If a debtor's estate is subject to a "collective execution" in Italy, territoriality will prevail. There should then be separate adjudications of insolvency in each nation where there are assets.

If there are insolvency proceedings in Italy, a foreign creditor may prove in those proceedings because all creditors are equal under Italian law and no particular rules apply to foreign creditors. A creditor may prove his debt in multiple bankruptcies but Italian law seeks to ensure that the creditor will not gain any advantage.

4. Examples

Truosolo v Interchange Bank (Tribunal of Milan, 10 March 1969 and Court of Appeals of Milan, 6 March 1970)

This involved the recognition of a Swiss bankruptcy. An Italian creditor, an attorney, made a claim to the Italian assets on the grounds of preference and argued against the recognition of a Swiss adjudication of bankruptcy in Italy on the grounds that it violated Italian public policy. The creditor claimed:

- Swiss bankruptcy law did not recognise a preference of the sort claimed by him; and
- an Italian creditor could not bring proceedings against the Swiss bankrupt in Switzerland.

No exequatur was granted and the Italian creditor was entitled to payment out of the Italian assets before the foreign administrator.

Storper v Fallimento Storper (Tribunal of Bologna, 25 February 1966)

A New York company had an associated office in Italy which had been created without following the requirements of Italian law for the creation of a branch of a foreign corporation.

At first instance, an individual acting as agent of the New York corporation in Italy was declared bankrupt but this was reversed. The court held that the representative was an employee and therefore could not be an entrepreneur and could not be subject to separate bankruptcy proceedings, even though an individual acting as agent of a foreign corporation has unlimited liability for its corporate obligations pursuant to the Civil Code, article 2508. The court held that the foreign branch could not be adjudicated bankrupt as this would be contrary to the principal of unity. The Italian court felt that the American administrator should have petitioned the Italian courts for an exequatur of the New York bankruptcy order. Since this did not happen, the Italian court declared both the New York company and then the Italian branch bankrupt.

Chapter 21

JAPAN

1. Under general law

A foreign judgment may be recognised if a Japanese court renders an "execution judgment" in favour of the foreign claimant. The Code of Civil Procedure (CCP), article 200, sets out several prerequisites for recognition. The most important of these is reciprocity. There will be no re-examination of the facts of a particular case if the prerequisites are satisfied. The Supreme Court apparently takes a relatively flexible approach when considering the reciprocity requirement and will consider it satisfied if the important points for recognition and enforcement of foreign judgments between Japan and the foreign country are essentially similar.

Once the execution judgment is obtained, the enforcement procedure is similar to that for domestic judgments. In the past, the Japanese courts have permitted enforcement of judgments rendered in several states of the United States, Switzerland, and Germany.

However, a foreign insolvency order is not deemed to be a foreign judgment which can be recognised and enforced in Japan under CCP, article 200.

2. Assisting legislation

There is no assisting legislation for access and recognition of a foreign administrator.

Japanese laws governing recognition and enforcement of foreign insolvency orders are based on principles of strict territoriality and not comity. The Bankruptcy Act 1922, article 3(2) provides that a foreign insolvency order shall not be effective against property situate in Japan and a Japanese insolvency order shall only affect the debtor's Japanese assets. Other insolvency statutes, including the Corporate Reorganisation Act 1951, have similar provisions.

3. Insolvency practice

Although strict territoriality is the theory under the statutory provisions mentioned above, in practice the Japanese courts have shown signs of applying principles of universality.

The Japanese court which has jurisdiction over a debtor is that where the debtor's legal seat or major place of business is located, or, failing this, where the debtor has a business location and assets.

Following the strict rules of territoriality, the Japanese courts cannot extend their jurisdiction over a debtor's assets located in a foreign country. However, the provisions of the Bankruptcy Act and the Corporate Reorganisation Act 1951 do not deprive Japanese administrators of their power to take control of debtors' assets in foreign jurisdictions. Recent case law indicates that a Japanese administrator may be required to recover and preserve foreign assets utilising foreign insolvency systems.

Whether the Japanese courts will recognise the effect of foreign insolvency proceedings in Japan in practice has not yet been determined because, up to 1992, no Japanese court received a request for judicial co-operation from a foreign court. However, the status of a foreign administrator, and his power to represent a foreign debtor in Japan who is subject to foreign insolvency proceedings, has been recognised by the courts in Japan in that the Tokyo Court of Appeal has held that a foreign administrator was entitled to bring any action in Japan on behalf of the debtor with regard to property located in Japan.

A foreign administrator is enabled to take control of and dispose of the debtor's moveable assets located in Japan and collect debts owed to the debtor in Japan. If a person in possession of the moveable assets refuses to hand them over, or if a person indebted to the debtor refuses to pay the debt then the administrator may take proceedings against that person.

If the debtor is not co-operative in transferring land, buildings and other assets located in Japan, then the foreign administrator may sue the debtor in Japan, requiring him to file any relevant documents with the registration office of the court of competent jurisdiction to transfer the title of the property to the administrator or a person designated by the administrator.

If a creditor seeks to attack the debtor's Japanese assets individually or if the debtor refuses to co-operate, the administrator is entitled to file a petition for bankruptcy in Japan.

If there are Japanese creditors, Japanese courts will allow insolvency proceedings to be commenced in Japan which are concurrent with foreign insolvency proceedings. This may be necessary where there have been antecedent transactions, as a foreign administrator cannot attack antecedent transactions: only an administrator appointed in Japanese proceedings is allowed by Japanese law to exercise that power.

A foreign creditor has the same status as a Japanese creditor and is able to file claims with the Japanese courts for distribution purposes and his claim will rank on an equal basis with local claims. There is no precedent which authorises the foreign administrator to file claims on behalf of the foreign creditors.

There are significant practical problems in applying for recognition by the Japanese courts:

- Recovery of assets in Japan requires precise details of those assets to be provided including evidence of the location, value and ownership. It can be difficult and costly to obtain sufficiently precise information, especially as companies' assets are generally subject to prior charges;
- It is easy for a Japanese debtor to assign his assets. A written notarised deed of assignment is binding on all third parties whether or not they have notice of it. The assignment will be effective if made before notice of any order relating to the assets is received by the debtor;
- The costs may be prohibitive if there are few assets in the foreign bankruptcy estate. This is because, even if a foreign administrator wins an action, his costs would not include his legal fees because everyone is presumed to be able to represent himself in Japan; and
- It is often difficult to find a local lawyer who is not already retained by a Japanese defendant company.

Some authorities suggest that where a Japanese defendant is a company and there are problems in establishing the whereabouts of its assets, a foreign administrator may attempt to attack the personal assets of the company's officers and the resulting inconvenience will in practice give considerable leverage. We cannot vouch for the legality or effectiveness of this tactic.

4. Examples

Tokyo Kosei 30 January 1981

The Japanese court recognised a Swiss administrator's rights over a debtor's Japanese assets. The debtor was a Swiss corporation and the administrator was permitted to litigate to recover the debtor's rights to its Japanese trade mark against a Japanese creditor which had obtained an attachment over it.

SAS Nagoya District Court number 91 of 1991

The Court appointed an additional administrator to dispose of a company's foreign assets, while the first-appointed administrator dealt with the domestic assets. The company's petition for the execution of a judgment was acknowledged and reorganisations of the French subsidiary companies were supervised by the Japanese courts in the course of the liquidation of the subsidiary Japanese company.

Re Maruko Number 1 of 1991 Heisei 3

The court allowed a Japanese administrator to file a petition for domestic United States bankruptcy administration under the United States Federal Bankruptcy Code, section 303, aimed at a full-scale reorganisation, instead of commencing ancillary proceedings under section 304 because the estate involved considerable real estate in the United States. The United States court abstained from including the Japanese assets under section 305. (A similar decision was given in *Re Ken International (Hu) No 1594 of 1991* Heisei 3.)

Chapter 22

JERSEY

1. Under general law

Prior to the implementation of the Bankruptcy (Désastre) (Jersey) Law 1990 (the Bankruptcy Law) the Royal Court of Jersey applied general principles of judicial comity in exercising its inherent jurisdiction to deal with applications by foreign administrators for access and recognition. Comity remains an important principle for the Royal Court.

A foreign claimant or foreign administrator may gain access to, and the recognition of, the Royal Court by:

- registering the judgment of a foreign court in the Royal Court under the Judgment (Reciprocal Enforcement) (Jersey) Law 1960; or
- commencing proceedings in Jersey in his own name, essentially by way of the issue of an Order of Justice (Writ) through the intermediacy of Jersey counsel.

Any democratic country whose insolvency laws are based on the principles of universality and equality, which is willing to grant reciprocal treatment to Jersey, will qualify for assistance.

2. Assisting legislation

The Bankruptcy Law, Article 48, empowers the Royal Court to assist the courts of other prescribed territories in all matters relating to the insolvency of any person to the extent that it thinks fit. The Bankruptcy (Désastre) (Jersey) Rules 1991, (the Bankruptcy Rules) rule 11(4), prescribes the countries for the purposes of Article 48 and as at December 1994 the following had been prescribed:

– Australia;
– Guernsey;
– The Isle of Man; and
– United Kingdom.

The assistance given by the Royal Court is discretionary and the Court will pay particular regard to the rules of private international law.

A letter of request is issued out of the foreign court and presented by Jersey counsel to the Royal Court. The Royal Court will exercise any jurisdiction it, or the requesting court, could exercise domestically including:

– endorsing and registering the appointment of the foreign administrator;
– the Viscount, the executive officer of the Royal Court, may be appointed to render appropriate assistance to the administrator and
– information may be made available by discovery of documents or the examination of witnesses.

The limitations on Article 48 are:

– the Royal Court will not enforce payment of foreign revenue debts as this is contrary to the rules of private international law;
– the enforcement must not offend the principles of universality and equality to which Jersey bankruptcy law subscribes; and
– there must be reciprocity from the foreign courts.

3.   Insolvency practice

While the Bankruptcy Law, Article 48 envisages the provision of ancillary juris-diction, there are limitations. If a debtor in a Jersey bankruptcy has carried on business in Jersey but has a principal place of business elsewhere, the Viscount would be primarily responsible for realising the debtor's assets, wherever situ-ate, due to the application of the principle of universality set out in the Bankruptcy Law. This might bring the Viscount in conflict with concurrent administration procedures. The Royal Court could offer ancillary jurisdiction to a foreign administrator provided the principle of equality of treatment of credi-tors is not prejudiced and the Viscount is not hindered in the conduct of the Jersey Désastre.

Countries which "ring fence" local assets for the benefit of local creditors or whose insolvency proceedings do not have extra-territorial effect would be unlikely to receive extensive ancillary assistance and may not qualify for pre-scription under the Bankruptcy Rules, rule 11(4).

4. Examples

Re Tucker (1987–1988) JLR 473

Re Royco Investment Company Ltd 1 June 1989

The Royal Court consented to receive the declaration "*en désastre*" of the moveable property of Royco upon the application of the English Provisional Liquidator.

The English Trustee obtained an order from the English High Court requesting that the Royal Court act in aid of, or be auxiliary to, it (as provided for under the Bankruptcy Act 1914, Section 122) in ordering the production of documents by, and the private examination of, the bankrupt's legal representative in Jersey. The Trustee's action was funded by the Inland Revenue who were the only effective creditor.

The Royal Court could exercise its discretion and refuse to grant aid notwithstanding the mandatory wording of section 122, because section 122 operated subject to general public policy. For example, the Jersey courts will not enforce foreign revenue laws. The request for assistance amounted to an indirect attempt to enforce foreign revenue laws and the Royal Court had no jurisdiction to grant the request.

In re State of Norway 1990 1 AC 723

In re Walkers Advertising Associates Ltd 21 December 1992 (Unreported)

In re R v Charlton and others 19 November 1993 (Unreported)

Chapter 23

MEXICO

1. Under general law

Provided it is not contrary to Mexican law, any foreign judgment may be recognised and enforced in Mexico, subject to any treaties and conventions to which Mexico is a party.

Once certain formal requirements are satisfied, a foreign judgment will be recognised by a Mexican court and thereafter it may be enforced. The formal requirements are:

- the letter of request sent by the foreign court must be in accordance with formalities required by Mexican law;
- the foreign judgment must have originated from an action *in personam* and not an action *in rem*;
- the foreign court must have had jurisdiction to hear the case;
- the foreign proceedings should have been duly served on the debtor;
- the judgment should be final and conclusive;
- enforcement of the judgment should not be contrary to Mexican law; and
- the judgment should be properly authenticated.

The court will not look into the merits of the foreign judgment but retains discretion to grant enforcement.

2. Assisting legislation

Mexico is a signatory to the following International Conventions:

- Interamerican Convention on the Extraterritorial Effectiveness of Foreign Judgments and Arbitral Awards, Montevideo, Uruguay, 8 May 1979;

- Interamerican Convention on International Jurisdiction for the Extra-territorial Effectiveness of Foreign Judgments and Arbitral Awards, La Paz, Bolivia, 24 May 1984; and
- Agreement between the United Mexican States and the Kingdom of Spain on the recognition and enforcement of civil and commercial judgments and awards, Madrid, Spain, 17 April 1989.

It is not clear whether any of these have provisions specifically dealing with recognition and enforcement of foreign bankruptcy orders.

3. Insolvency practice

A Mexican court will recognise a foreign bankruptcy order only if it is satisfied that the order substantially complies with the local law on bankruptcy and suspension of payments.

Foreign creditors have the right to prove their claims in local bankruptcy proceedings.

A Mexican court has jurisdiction to declare foreign individuals resident in Mexico or foreign companies carrying on business in Mexico bankrupt. The Mexican bankruptcy order will affect all assets of the bankrupt situated in Mexico.

4. Examples

None known.

Chapter 24

THE NETHERLANDS

1. Under general law

Dutch insolvency proceedings are based on the principle of territoriality, because bankruptcy is regarded as a form of execution that is an act of sovereignty. The principle of universality of bankruptcy is, however, embodied in the Dutch Bankruptcy Act (Faillissementswet) 1893 (the Dutch Act), as this prescribes that a bankruptcy in Holland comprises all the assets of the bankrupt wherever they are situated.

A foreign bankruptcy does not prevent attachment of the debtor's assets located in the Netherlands. The assets in the Netherlands will not be transferred to the foreign forum, even following a formal request by the foreign administrator, and local creditors are free to bring individual actions to satisfy claims against the debtor's assets.

A Dutch court may declare a person bankrupt in the Netherlands notwithstanding the existence of foreign bankruptcy proceedings. Any creditor, regardless of nationality or domicile, can petition for the bankruptcy of a debtor.

2. Assisting legislation

The Dutch Act contains no provision for the recognition of foreign insolvency proceedings or foreign administrators. There is no legislation requiring a Dutch court to co-operate with a foreign court or foreign administrator.

Foreign bankruptcy orders are only recognised under specific treaties providing for the recognition and enforcement of such orders. Only the Treaty of 28 March 1925 between the Netherlands and Belgium (which governs territorial jurisdiction, bankruptcy and the authority and execution of judgment, arbitral awards and notarial acts between the Netherlands and Belgium), provides for mutual recognition and enforcement of bankruptcy proceedings. Its effects are limited to decisions originating in these countries.

The Hague Evidence Convention of 1970 can be utilised in bankruptcy matters to obtain judicial co-operation: Article 1 enables a foreign court using the letter of request procedure to request the assistance of the competent authority of another state in obtaining evidence or performing some other judicial acts.

The Netherlands is a party to other treaties which provide for the enforcement of foreign judgments but these explicitly exclude insolvency proceedings.

3. Insolvency practice

A foreign administrator must rely on general civil procedures to obtain possession of real or personal property and to collect receivables. Foreign bankruptcy proceedings other than orders made in Belgium do not lead to an automatic stay in respect of the bankrupt's assets.

Notwithstanding the overwhelming principle of territoriality, foreign bankruptcy proceedings are given limited recognition: if a bankruptcy is validly and legally opened in a foreign state, the foreign administrator will be recognised in the Netherlands in respect of the assets located in the foreign state provided these foreign bankruptcy proceedings do not violate or infringe Dutch law.

Recently the Dutch courts appear to be adopting a more purposive approach to the interpretation of Dutch bankruptcy law and the recognition offered as a result to foreign administrators.

Therefore a foreign administrator may now find it easier to be recognised by the Dutch courts because constitutive status judgments have been recognised by the courts (Judgment of 24 November 1916, H R; N J 1917). Hence, a foreign administrator may have the *locus standi* to represent a bankrupt and authority to bring or defend legal actions provided that the laws in the state where he was appointed vest all the bankrupt's rights in the administrator or imply that the administrator can legally act in lieu of, or on behalf of, the bankrupt. An action in the foreign administrator's jurisdiction which has effect in the Netherlands may be accepted if it does not require any form of execution. (Judgment of the Dutch Supreme Court of 23 February 1917, HRNJ 1917, 347, President of the Breda District Court 30 March 1983, NJ 1984, 798, District Court of Arnhem, 4 January 1976, 445.)

If a foreign debtor has a branch in the Netherlands, foreign bankruptcy proceedings do not automatically affect the operations or the assets of the branch. It may be the subject of separate Dutch bankruptcy proceedings under the supervision of the Dutch court and with the appointment of a Dutch administrator, but these proceedings would claim universal effect.

The validity of a foreign creditor's claim is determined by Dutch private international law. A foreign creditor's claim is not subordinated to that of a local creditor in Dutch bankruptcy proceedings.

A foreign administrator will not be able to attack antecedent transactions either under the laws of his own jurisdiction or under the Dutch Act, article 42ff, because the Dutch avoidance laws can be invoked only by persons recognised by the law as having a standing to bring such actions. However, since Dutch courts recognise constitutive judgments, a foreign administrator may be able to seek to avoid antecedent transactions using non-bankruptcy law, provided such action does not prejudice the interests of bona fide third parties in the Netherlands.

4. Examples

Arcalon BV & Ramar BV v USA Bankruptcy Court for the Southern District of California **(NJ (1987) No 149) (A decision of the Supreme Court of The Hague)**

The Dutch courts co-operated with the American Bankruptcy Court by giving a broad interpretation to Article 1 of the Hague Evidence Convention. The United States Bankruptcy Court, by a letter of request, applied under Article 1 to the District Court of Hague seeking access to two witnesses residing in the Netherlands and requesting certain documents be produced. The District Court held that the letter of request complied with Article 1 and allowed the execution of the request on the assumption that the aim of the requested assistance was to provide the foreign administrator with means to obtain information about the bankrupt's estate. The Dutch trustees in bankruptcy appealed against this decision to the Court of Appeal in Amsterdam (which upheld the decision of the District Court) and then to the Supreme Court.

The Supreme Court had to decide whether or not the letter of request complied with the provisions of Article 1 paragraph 2. The Supreme Court observed that the nature and purpose of the Convention is to promote co-operation between states and therefore Article 1 should be broadly interpreted. On that basis, the Court held that the administration and winding-up of the estate of a bankrupt under the supervision of a judicial authority can be regarded in the context of a bankruptcy pronounced by such authority or by another judicial authority as "proceedings" within the meaning of Article 1 paragraph 2. The broad interpretation of Article 1 enabled the Dutch Court to co-operate with the American Bankruptcy Court.

Chapter 25

NEW ZEALAND

1. Under general law

New Zealand is based on English common law, although now the New Zealand courts refer to decisions of the English, American and Canadian courts.

Where there is no specific statute governing the recognition and enforcement of judgments of a foreign country, such judgments may only be enforced under the common law rules. It appears that a New Zealand court will not enforce a foreign judgment based only on the principle of comity of nations. If a foreign judgment is to be enforced at common law, the foreign judgment creditor must sue on the foreign judgment in the New Zealand High Court. It cannot be directly enforced. If the action is successful, the Court will make an order whereby the judgment may be enforced as a local judgment against the judgment debtor and his property in New Zealand.

Where an enforcement action on a foreign judgment *in personam* has been filed, the New Zealand court must first be satisfied that the jurisdiction of the foreign court granting the judgment is recognised by New Zealand law. The judgment should be final and conclusive and for a debt or a definite sum of money.

If the foreign judgment in question is a judgment *in rem*, a New Zealand court will treat the judgment as final and conclusive and binding between parties.

If the aforesaid criteria are satisfied, a New Zealand court may make an order in favour of the foreign judgment creditor. The court will not re-examine the merits of the case or entertain a defence to the effect that the judgment was given as a result of an error of fact or law. The only defences available to the defendant are that the foreign judgment was obtained by fraud or that its enforcement would be contrary to New Zealand public policy. In *NZ Marine Services Ltd* v *Bohon*, Barker ACJ noted that policy leans in favour of recognising the judgments of the courts of reciprocal countries (even if the New Zealand court may be unhappy about the basis of the judgment) (See Butterworths Current Law, October 1993).

Non-insolvency judgments of certain foreign countries will be enforced after they have been registered under the Reciprocal Enforcement of Judgments Act 1934 (REJ) or the Judicature Act 1980, section 56. The latter section will apply only in respect of judgments that are not enforceable under the provisions of the REJ.

A debtor's moveable property, wherever situate, is governed by the law of the country in which he is domiciled. Thus, if the debtor is adjudicated bankrupt in his country of domicile the right to all his property in New Zealand will also pass to the foreign administrator. In such a situation, upon a request being made by the foreign administrator, the court has the discretion to make an order for the delivery of the property in New Zealand to the administrator. However, the court will make such an order only after a local court has confirmed that the foreign bankruptcy can be recognised as a valid bankruptcy which passes title to the foreign administrator.

A debtor's immoveable property is governed by the law of the country where the land is situate. If the land is situate in New Zealand, a local court may assist a foreign administrator to realise the immoveable property by appointing a local receiver of the property for the purpose of collecting rents and profits, or by ordering the sale of the property for the benefit of the creditors.

2.   Assisting legislation

The Insolvency Act 1967, section 135 provides that:

- The Supreme Court shall, in all matters of bankruptcy, act in aid of and be auxiliary to any court of a Commonwealth country other than New Zealand, being a court having jurisdiction in bankruptcy, and an order of that court requesting aid shall be sufficient to enable the Supreme Court to exercise in regard to the matter specified in the order such powers as the Supreme Court might exercise in respect of the matter if it had arisen within its own jurisdiction.
- The Court may, if it thinks fit, exercise the power specified in subsection (1) of this section at the request of the court in any country that is not a Commonwealth country.

The procedure involves a letter of request being issued from a foreign court requesting aid in an insolvency matter. Where aid is requested from a court of a Commonwealth country it is mandatory for the High Court in New Zealand to exercise its powers and assist the court of the Commonwealth country. However, it has the discretion whether or not to do so if the request is made by any other court.

In New Zealand the bankruptcy rules apply in the winding-up of insolvent companies. The Companies Act 1955, section 307 and the Companies Act 1993, section 302 provide that in the winding-up of an insolvent company the same rules shall prevail as are in force under the law of bankruptcy.

If a foreign company has a place of business in New Zealand either as a registered or unregistered company, winding-up proceedings must be commenced in the New Zealand High Court (Companies Act 1993, section 342).

The initiation of winding-up proceedings of a registered or unregistered company in New Zealand involves an application to the High Court under the Companies Act 1955, section 263 (previously section 218). Companies falling under the Companies Act 1993 may be wound up pursuant to section 289.

3. Insolvency practice

The assistance and recognition which the New Zealand courts will actually give is uncertain because there have been few instances when the courts in New Zealand have had to decide on issues such as recognition of foreign insolvencies and foreign administrators, the powers of foreign administrators to deal with property in New Zealand or whether to assist foreign courts.

Where concurrent bankruptcies are taking place in different countries, it has been suggested that a New Zealand court may adopt either of the possible solutions enunciated in the English case *Re Artola Hermanos, ex parte Chale* [1890] 24 QBD 640.

First, each forum could administer the assets situate within its jurisdiction, and allow all creditors, wherever resident, to prove claims. The "hotchpotch" rule will be applied to produce equality between creditors as far as possible. The Court was aware that in such a situation, the inconvenience of double and triple proofs may occur, but took the view that this would be less inconvenient than the inconveniences created by any other course. Further, following the House of Lords decision in *Ewing* v *Orr Ewing* (9 App Cases 34) the Court stated that the forum in which the assets are located will have jurisdiction to administer those assets, although it may be that the law of domicile will govern the mode of distribution; or

Secondly, every other foreign forum could yield to the forum of domicile, and act only as an accessory of, and in aid to, the forum of domicile.

However, current practice appears to be that if foreign bankruptcy proceedings are recognised by the New Zealand High Court the foreign administrator will be accorded recognition but a local New Zealand administrator will be appointed. The New Zealand aspects of the foreign administration will be vested in the New Zealand administrator. The foreign administrator will deal with the matter through the New Zealand administrator.

Foreign bankruptcy orders will be recognised in New Zealand provided that the orders are proved to have been made in the foreign jurisdiction and that the foreign jurisdiction was sufficiently connected with the insolvent person or company and properly exercised. However, the foreign order is not directly enforceable in New Zealand. A concurrent order must be obtained under the procedures for individual bankruptcy set out under the Insolvency Act 1967, section 135, the Companies Act 1955, section 307 and the Companies Act 1993, section 302. The nature and extent of the aid is at the discretion of the New Zealand High Court. Proper and valid claims in New Zealand may have priority over claims in the foreign bankruptcy.

The process of winding-up a foreign company by a foreign court will be recognised in New Zealand if proved to have taken place abroad and if the foreign court requests recognition of those proceedings or judicial assistance based on those proceedings.

The foreign proceedings will be an influential factor for the New Zealand courts to allow ancillary proceedings to be issued and to enable the appointment of a New Zealand administrator to assist the foreign administrator. The ancillary proceedings will give effect to the winding-up.

4. Examples

Re Grose (High Court, Christchurch, B 404/92, 21 September 1992)

In this case concurrent bankruptcies were proceeding in Australia and New Zealand. The applicant, the Australian Administrator and the Federal Court, sought the aid of the High Court in New Zealand under the Insolvency Act 1967, section 35. Making the order for aid, the New Zealand Court required the claims in the New Zealand bankruptcy to be met by the property realised in New Zealand before the balance, if any, was made available to Australian creditors. (see Laws of New Zealand, 1994 para 557, footnote 7.)

Re Beadle, HC Auckland, B No 116/80, 20 August 1980 (Judgment: 1 September 1930)

The action arose by way of a letter of request to the High Court in Auckland from the Supreme Court of Queensland, the latter of which court exercises federal jurisdiction in bankruptcy. The letter of request represented to the Supreme Court that the New Zealand property of the insolvent be made available to the Official Receiver in Queensland, to be dealt with by him in accordance with the Australian bankruptcy laws.

Barker J granted the letter of request stating:

"Counsel for Official Assignee submitted that although the word 'shall' is used in section 135, the power of the Court is discretionary since there is, for example, a reluctance of the courts of one state to enforce the revenue laws of another state . . . I think Counsel is correct; in the present case, there is no matter shown which would deter this Court from giving effect to the comity and reciprocity which should exist between courts of comparable status exercising similar jurisdiction in Commonwealth countries."

Gordon Pacific Developments v *Conlon* (1993, 3 New Zealand Law Reports 765)

The plaintiff sought to enforce a judgment of the District Court of Queensland, Australia, in New Zealand under the Judicature Act 1908. Since Australia is a Commonwealth country, Henry J ruled that the REJ was applicable. Enforcement was refused on the ground that, since the judgment was a judgment *in personam* the jurisdictional requirements set out in section 6 of the Act were not satisfied. Therefore the jurisdiction of the Queensland Court could not be recognised.

Chapter 26

NIGERIA

1. Under general law

Nigerian law is derived from English law, local statute and precedent.

There are two ways in which a judgment or order of a foreign court may, in theory, be recognised and enforced in Nigeria.

First, under statute: the Foreign Judgments (Reciprocal Enforcement) Act (Cap 152, Laws of the Federation of Nigeria, 1990) (FJRE) is the principal statute governing enforcement and recognition. The High Court will permit the registration of a foreign judgment if certain criteria are satisfied. Of these, reciprocity is the most important. Once registered the foreign judgment has the same effect as a Nigerian judgment.

FJRE, section 3 authorises the Minister of Justice to extend the application of this Act to judgments given in a superior court of any country, provided substantial reciprocity is assured by the foreign court for judgments given in the Supreme Courts of Nigeria. So far the Act has not been extended to any foreign country.

Secondly, under common law: a Nigerian court may accord recognition if the foreign judgment is final and conclusive and the foreign court was competent to hear the case. Enforcement of a foreign judgment is initiated by filing an action in Nigeria based on the foreign judgment. Comity has been suggested as a basis for enforcement and recognition but there does not appear to be any authority on this point. Conversely, it has been held that where a foreign judgment is sought to be recognised and enforced at common law, the question of reciprocity does not arise.

Statute prevails over common law and thus a creditor may only seek recognition and enforcement of a foreign judgment at common law if statute does not prohibit this.

Foreign creditors and litigants are able to use Nigerian courts relatively easily provided that the courts accept jurisdiction for a particular matter. Access to

Nigerian courts is underlined by the 1979 Constitution of the Federal Republic of Nigeria.

2. Assisting legislation

The Nigerian Bankruptcy Act 1979 is based on English law, but it is unclear whether or not it contains a similar provision to the English Insolvency Act 1986, section 426.

3. Insolvency practice

In practice it appears that the most reliable method of having a foreign judgment recognised and enforced in Nigeria is at common law; by filing an action based on the foreign judgment.

A foreign bankruptcy order will be recognised in Nigeria, because such an order relates to an individual's status. It will therefore be recognised like any other foreign judgment, provided the required criteria are satisfied.

It may be noted that the Nigerian courts have jurisdiction to bankrupt any person who commits an act of bankruptcy in Nigeria. Thus, a foreign person maybe adjudged bankrupt. The Bankruptcy Act 1979 (Cap 30, Laws of the Federation of Nigeria, 1990) governs the bankruptcy of individuals and companies will be wound up under the Companies Act 1968 (Cap 59, Laws of the Federation of Nigeria, 1990).

4. Examples

Alfred C Toepfer Inc v Edokpolor (Trading as John Edokpolor & Sons) (1965, All Nigerian Law Reports p 292)

The Supreme Court held that a party who is not prevented by the Foreign Judgments (Reciprocal Enforcement) Act of 1960, section 8, from suing upon a foreign judgment is entitled to sue on it regardless of whether there is reciprocal treatment in the country where it was obtained.

Chapter 27

PHILIPPINES

1. Under general law

A foreign judgment may be recognised in the Philippines, if:

- it arises out of civil or commercial proceedings;
- it is a final judgment;
- it is consistent with fundamental principles of public policy; and
- it is not tainted by fraud.

The foreign judgment gives rise to cause of action and enforcement proceedings may be commenced in the Philippines by filing a new complaint.

2. Assisting legislation

None known.

3. Insolvency practice

Foreign individuals and companies with legal capacity to carry on business in the Philippines are subject to Philippine insolvency law and the Philippine bankruptcy court has jurisdiction in the bankruptcy of such foreign persons.

There are two views as to the practice which will be adopted by the Philippine courts in recognising and enforcing foreign bankruptcy orders.

The first is that it is considered presumptive evidence of the rights established as a result of the bankruptcy order between the debtor, his creditors and the foreign administrator. The foreign bankruptcy order may only be challenged by establishing lack of jurisdiction on the part of the court making the order, lack of notice to the bankrupt, collusion, fraud or mistake of law or fact.

The second, and minority view, is based on reciprocity. If a judgment of a Philippine court is regarded by a foreign court as conclusive on its merits, foreign bankruptcy orders from that jurisdiction are considered conclusive in the Philippines (*see Ingenohol* v *Olsen & Co*).

4. Examples

Ingenohol v *Olsen & Co*

Chapter 28

POLAND

1. Under general law

The Code of Civil Procedure 1964, article 1117 determines the *locus standi* of a foreign claimant.

Foreign claimants, presumably including foreign administrators, are treated in the same way as Polish creditors. This is backed up by a general principle of equality in Article 8. Reciprocity appears to be important.

2. Assisting legislation

None known.

3. Insolvency Practice

Where there is reciprocity, a foreign claimant may commence proceedings in Poland, acting by a foreign attorney notwithstanding that the attorney may not be entitled to practice in Poland otherwise.

Foreign claimants can claim, and file proofs of debt in Polish bankruptcies in the same manner as Polish creditors. However, from a procedural point of view, foreign claimants are obliged to provide the Polish administrator with addresses in Poland to which notices and correspondence may be sent. It is therefore advisable to retain professional advisers based in Poland.

4. Examples

None known.

Chapter 29

SCOTLAND

1. Under general law

Although Scotland is a separate jurisdiction from England and Northern Ireland and has its own courts, it is part of the United Kingdom and is influenced by English legislation to a material extent. The courts' attitude to comity is as recorded for England.

Foreign judgments may be enforced in Scotland through the use of various statutory procedures. The basis of these procedures is the registration of the foreign judgment in the records, known as "The Books", of the Scottish court, followed by enforcement as if it were a Scottish judgment. The problem of which judgments may be enforced can be complex. The common law procedure to enforce a foreign judgment is to seek a decree conform which is a procedure by way of summons. The case proceeds like an ordinary action for payment, but founded on the foreign judgment.

2. Assisting legislation

Courts having jurisdiction in relation to insolvency law in any part of the United Kingdom are obliged to assist courts having corresponding jurisdiction in the Channel Islands, the Isle of Man and any country or territory designated for this purpose by the Secretary of State in a statutory instrument (the Insolvency Act 1986, section 426 (1986 Act)). The countries and territories presently designated are Anguilla, Australia, The Bahamas, Bermuda, Botswana, Canada, Cayman Islands, Falkland Islands, Gibraltar, Guernsey, Hong Kong, Republic of Ireland, Malaysia, Montserrat, New Zealand, Republic of South Africa, St Helena, Turks and Caicos Islands, Tuvalu and Virgin Islands: Co-operation of Insolvency Courts (Designation of Relevant Countries and Territories) Order

1986) SI 1986/2123; Insolvency Act 1986 (Guernsey) Order 1989 SI 1989/2409 (per Stair on Companies, volume 4).

In the case of receivers, it is particularly provided that a receiver appointed under the law of any part of the United Kingdom in respect of property comprised in a charge, which as created was a floating charge, may exercise his powers in any other part of the United Kingdom, so far as that exercise is not inconsistent with the law applicable there.

The courts in England and Wales or in Scotland may refer the examination of witnesses in winding-up proceedings to another court in any part of the United Kingdom. Where an administration order has been made, an administrative receiver has been appointed, the company has gone into liquidation or a provisional liquidator has been appointed, the court may order any person who appears to have in his possession any property of the company to be examined in any part of the United Kingdom where that person may be, or in a place outside the United Kingdom. A warrant issued in exercise of any jurisdiction in relation to insolvency law in any part of the United Kingdom for the arrest of any person may be executed throughout the United Kingdom

The Court of Session has jurisdiction in any action by a creditor of a Scottish company against its liquidator, notwithstanding the domicile of the liquidator or wherever the loss occurred.

In exercising its discretion to apply the law of either relevant jurisdiction, the Scottish courts will have regard to rules of private international law (A E Anton, *Private International Law (2nd ed)* (1990) 274).

3. Insolvency practice

Where a foreign company is in liquidation in the place of its domicile, the Scottish courts will recognise the title of the foreign administrator to deal with the assets of the company situated in Scotland, but will not (apart from the exercise of discretion in relevant cases) apply the insolvency law of the foreign territory so as to defeat the rights of persons who have prior claims to those assets (*New Zealand Loan and Mercantile Agency Co* v *Morrison* [1898] AC 349, PC; *National Bank of Greece and Athens SA* v *Metliss* [1958] AC 509; [1957] 3 All E R 608 HL; *Felixstowe Dock & Railway Company* v *United States Lines Inc* 1989 QB 360; [1988] 2 All E R 77).

The fact that an overseas company is in liquidation in the place of its domicile, or has been dissolved, is not a bar to winding-up by the Scottish court under the 1986 Act. As a matter of Scottish law, a liquidator appointed by the Scottish courts in relation to an overseas company enjoys powers in relation to all the assets of the company, wherever situated, and is under a corresponding duty (*Re International Tin Council* [1987] Ch 419 at 446; [1987] 1 All E R 890 at 899), although the fact that other countries may not recognise the Scottish winding-up order imposes practical limitations on the consequences of the order.

Where the company is simultaneously being wound up in the country of incorporation, the Scottish court should seek to avoid unnecessary conflict and, so far as possible, ensure that the winding-up is conducted as ancillary to the principal liquidation. The court might authorise the liquidator to refrain from seeking to recover assets situated beyond the jurisdiction, thereby protecting him from any claim that he had been derelict in his duty.

A creditor of a Scottish company in liquidation in Scotland may be restrained by the court from enforcing his claim overseas if he is subject to the jurisdiction of the Scottish court *(Pacific Coast Mining Co Liquidators* v *Walker* (1886) 13 R 816; *California Redwood Company (In Liquidation)* v *Merchant Banking Co of London* (1886) 13 R 1202*)*. Jurisdiction may exist by virtue of the creditor having lodged a claim in the liquidation. A restraining order may be made under section 130 (2) of the Insolvency Act 1986 or at common law, although in England it has been held that this section does not apply to proceedings outside Great Britain (*Re Vocalion (Foreign) Ltd* [1932] 2 Ch 196).

4. Examples

None available

Chapter 30

SINGAPORE

1. Under general law

Singapore is a common law country. English cases are often followed and referred to by Singaporean judges and legislators have also been guided by English statues. However, the laws are by no means identical.

A foreign judgment has no direct operation in Singapore. However, foreign judgments may be recognised and enforced at common law or under statute.

At common law, the foreign claimant may apply to the High Court of Singapore for summary judgment under Order 14 of the Supreme Court Rules.

Once the existence of the foreign judgment is proved, the burden of proof lies with the defendant and the defences available to him under the rules of private international law are that:

- the foreign court was not competent to render the judgment due to the lack of proper jurisdiction;
- the foreign judgment was obtained by fraud; or
- the foreign judgment is contrary to public policy in Singapore.

Under statute, upon registration, certain foreign judgments will be recognised and enforced in Singapore on the basis of reciprocity. The relevant statutes are:

- The Reciprocal Enforcement of Commonwealth Judgments Act (Statutes of the Republic of Singapore, 1985 Revised Cap 264).

   This provides for the enforcement of money judgments in civil actions rendered by a superior court of the United Kingdom and Northern Ireland. The Minister of Law has a discretion to extend the application of this Act to any other Commonwealth country, and it now applies to the following countries: Australia, Negara Brunei Darussalam, Sri Lanka,

Hong Kong, India (except Jammu and Kashmir), Malaysia, New Zealand, Pakistan, Papua New Guinea and the Windward Islands.

– The Reciprocal Enforcement Of Foreign Judgments Act (Statutes of the Republic of Singapore, 1985 Revised Cap 265).

This Act provides for the enforcement of foreign judgments for the payment of compensation or damages in both civil and criminal actions where the judgments are given in a foreign country which gives Singaporean judgments reciprocal treatment. The Minister of Law should be satisfied that "substantial reciprocity will be assured" before extending the application of the Act to any country. No countries have yet been specified under this Act.

It is important to note that both these statutes require the assurance that the relevant foreign country would reciprocally enforce judgments of a Singaporean court.

The above statutes do not apply to foreign insolvency orders. Bankruptcies of individuals or partnerships are governed by the Bankruptcy Act (Statutes of the Republic of Singapore, 1995) and bankruptcies of companies are governed by the Companies Act (Statutes of the Republic of Singapore, 1990 Revised Cap 50).

It is generally accepted that the law of the place of incorporation of a company governs its existence and status (*Banque Internationale de Commerce de Petrograd* v *Goukassow* [1923] 2 KB 682). Thus if a foreign company is wound up in the jurisdiction where it was incorporated, a Singaporean court will recognise the foreign winding-up order. A winding-up order made by a court in a jurisdiction other than where the company was incorporated will not be recognised.

It may be noted, however, that the Companies Act, sections 350–354, provide for the winding-up of a foreign company. On the application of the principle in *Banque Internationale de Commerce de Petrograd* v *Gouskassow* it appears that such a winding-up order made by a Singaporean court will be effective only in Singapore.

2.   Assisting legislation

The Bankruptcy Act 1995, section 151 states that the High Court and its officers shall in all matters of bankruptcy and insolvency act in aid of, and be auxiliary to, the courts of Malaysia having jurisdiction in such matters, as long as the law of Malaysia provides reciprocal treatment to requests made by a competent court in Singapore. This provision also applies to "designated countries", which will in due course be specified by notification in the Gazette.

The Companies Act 1990 does not have a similar statutory provision.

Thus, if, due to his bankruptcy, a debtor's property is vested in the Official Assignee in Malaysia, any of his property situate in Singapore will vest in a Malaysian Official Assignee. The Singaporean courts must recognise the title of the Malaysian Official Assignee to the Singaporean property as if the debtor was adjudged bankrupt in Singapore. The above provisions would not be effective if a petition for bankruptcy proceedings had already been presented in Singapore although if the petition is dismissed, or withdrawn, the provisions will be effective. A Malaysian Official Assignee may sue and be sued in any court in Singapore in its official name.

Since the Singaporean courts will recognise a foreign winding-up order made against a company in the country where it was incorporated, any administrator appointed under that country's laws will be recognised in Singapore.

The company's property situate in Singapore does not automatically vest in the foreign administrator. The property can be vested only by a vesting order made by a Singapore court under the Companies Act, section 269. The foreign administrator of a company shall have the powers and duties of a local administrator, only until a Singaporean administrator is appointed (section 377(2)(b)).

3. Insolvency practice

As one of the newly-industrialised nations in East Asia, Singapore's economic policies are geared towards promoting foreign business. Although foreign companies are encouraged to conduct business in Singapore, the law does not appear as yet to be sufficiently comprehensive to deal with the complicated cross-frontier problems that may arise in the event of the insolvency of foreign companies.

There is a growing awareness of these problems and commentators are calling for the amendment of the law before the problems are aggravated.

However, there is no discrimination between a foreign creditor and a local creditor. Unless a foreign creditor is a secured creditor, he will rank *pari passu* with other unsecured creditors in proving a claim.

4. Examples

Re China Underwriters Life and General Insurance Company Ltd (1988) I Malaysian Law Journal 409, (HC) P

In this case the Official Receivers of China Insurance in Hong Kong applied to the High Court in Singapore for an order for examination of the defendants under the Singapore Companies Act, 1990 section 285. Dismissing the application, the Court held, *inter alia*, that it did not have jurisdiction to make the order requested because section 285 gives the Court powers only in respect of companies being wound up in Singapore. Consequently, it did not have jurisdiction to make an order relating to the winding-up abroad of a foreign company.

Chapter 31

SOUTH AFRICA

1. Under general law

South African law is based on a mixture of Roman-Dutch law and English common law. In particular, the Companies Acts are based on the latter. The concept of comity is recognised and the courts maintain a positive attitude towards the recognition and enforcement of foreign judgments.

The law makes a distinction between "recognition" and "enforcement" but South African law will allow the enforcement of a foreign-money judgment once it is recognised providing that:

- the foreign court has jurisdiction or international competence;
- the judgment is final and conclusive;
- the recognition and enforcement of the foreign judgment does not infringe public policy or the concept of natural justice; and
- it does not contravene the Protection of Business Act 1978, section 1 which states that foreign judgments will not be enforced and letters of request will not be acted upon without prior permission from the Minister of Economic Affairs.

The South African courts will not recognise or enforce a foreign judgment of a revenue or penal nature.

A South African court has a general discretion to recognise a foreign-insolvency order based on principles of comity. Broadly, the South African courts will consider whether to recognise a foreign insolvency order and a foreign administrator as and when the need arises. Certain factors will be taken into account; namely the court must be satisfied that the insolvent was domiciled in the jurisdiction of the foreign court. Where the insolvent was not so domiciled, the South African courts will not recognise that the foreign insolvency order has any extra-territorial effect. In *Re Estate Morris* (1907, TS 657), Innes CJ stated that the South African courts:

"applying the principles of the Roman-Dutch law, must lay down that sequestration decrees made in the country of domicile of the insolvent are entitled, up to a certain point, to extra-territorial recognition". (1907, TS 657)

2. Assisting legislation

There is no statutory provision that requires a local court to recognise foreign orders or to extend its co-operation to a foreign court.

3. Insolvency practice

In practice the South African court will exercise its discretion to make orders appropriate to the circumstances of the case.

For example, a foreign insolvency order may be recognised subject to conditions imposed by the South African courts for the protection of local creditors, including requiring a foreign administrator to provide security for the proper performance of his duties. Recognition of a foreign insolvency order does not automatically result in the debtor acquiring the status of "insolvent" under South African law (*Herman NO* v *Tebb* 1929, CPD 65 at 72). The debtor may even be sued in the local courts by his foreign creditors (*Hymore Durban (Pty) Ltd* v *Gin Nin Weaving Factory* 1959, (1) SA 180 at 182). In other cases, it may be appropriate for South African insolvency proceedings to be opened to run in tandem with the foreign proceedings.

A foreign administrator is allowed to deal with the debtor's assets in South Africa, to convene statutory meetings and to investigate the debtor's affairs. His power to deal with property depends on whether the property is moveable or immoveable. The general rule is that an insolvency order made by the court of the state where the debtor is domiciled will automatically divest the insolvent of his moveable property in South Africa. Innes CJ explains this rule as follows:

"It is clear, more especially by our law, that sequestration at the domicile vests in the trustee of the insolvent all the latter's moveables, wherever situated. By a fiction of law the insolvent's moveable property is all considered to be present at his domicile, and sequestration there operates at once to transfer that moveable property, wherever it is actually situated." In *Re Estate Morris* (1907, TS 657)

The foreign administrator, therefore, may administer the moveable assets without making a formal application to the South African court for recognition of his appointment. The rationale for this rule is that it encourages the convenience of establishing a single administration. In practice, however, an application for formal recognition is invariably made and the need for formal recognition has become accepted (*Leslie's Trustee* v *Leslies* 1903 TS 839; *Ex parte Sewell's Curator* 1906, TS 195).

A foreign administrator cannot deal with the insolvent's immoveable property situate in South Africa unless the court formally recognises the foreign order appointing him. Granting recognition to a foreign administrator to deal with an insolvent's immoveable property in South Africa is a matter for the local court's discretion. This discretion is absolute but recognition is usually granted in the interests of comity and convenience. In *Ex parte B Z Stegmann* (1902 TS 40). Innes JP, while accepting the above rule, went on to state:

> "But on the other hand, the same court, acting from motives of comity or convenience, is equally justified in allowing the order of the judge of the domicile to operate within its jurisdiction, and in assisting the execution or enforcement of such order. The matter is entirely one for its own discretion. It seems clear, therefore, on the highest authority, that the judges of the various provinces of the Netherlands, while adhering to the rules that real property could only be dealt with by the law of the place where it was situated, had in any particular case the power, on the grounds of comity, to waive the right of insisting on this strict legal rule."

4. Examples

Moolman v *Builders and Developers (Pty) Ltd*—(1) SA 954

The appellant was the provisional liquidator of a company incorporated in the Republic of Transkei which had been placed in provisional liquidation by the Supreme Court of Transkei. The appellant obtained an order from the Transkei court to appoint a commissioner to interrogate the sole director and major shareholder of the company but the director objected to interrogation; whereupon the appellant applied to the local court for an order recognising his appointment as provisional liquidator and the order of the Transkei court relating to the appointment of the commissioner. The application was refused.

On appeal, reversing the lower court decision, it was held that the court had discretion whether or not to grant recognition and that the sole grounds for granting recognition were comity and convenience. It further held that the discretion in this case should have been exercised in the applicant's favour and the application for recognition granted. The court stated:

> "the foreign trustee derives his authority entirely from his appointment in a foreign country and is precluded from exercising the statutory powers of a locally-appointed provisional liquidator. The commissioner appointed by the Transkei court is in the same position; although he is at liberty to conduct the examination at a venue in South Africa and to examine witnesses who are prepared to submit to interrogation,

there is no means by which he, or any one else, can compel their attendance or oblige them to submit to interrogation if they are not prepared to do so. It is clear therefore that neither the appellant nor the commissioner will be able to perform their functions in South Africa without the active assistance of the court, which is what a recognition order entails".

Priestly v Clegg (1985 (3) 950)

The applicant, a trustee in bankruptcy appointed in England, applied for an order from the South African court recognising his appointment and empowering him to administer the estate in respect of all assets of the respondent situated in South Africa. The respondent argued that, as the major creditor of the insolvent's estate was the Commissioner of Inland Revenue in England, the application was in reality for the enforcement of the revenue laws of another country.

The court held that the rule relied on by the respondent did not apply where a liquidator or an official assignee or, as in this case, the trustee of an insolvent's estate, sought to get in property which would in due course of administration benefit ordinary creditors as well as the Revenue. The Australian decision in *Re Ayers, ex parte Evans* (51 FLR 395 & 56 FLR 235—see report for Australia) was considered at length.

Ex parte Palmer No: In Re Hahn (1993 (3) SA 359)

The applicant argued that a South African court may, on the basis of comity and convenience, grant recognition to a foreign administrator regardless of any consideration given to the insolvent's domicile. Dismissing the application the court held that the "bold assertion" that recognition simply involves an exercise of discretion based on considerations of comity and convenience could not be upheld. Berman J held:

"Comity and convenience is a factor which plays a part in influencing the local court to exercise its discretion in favour of recognising a foreign trustee; it is not a separate ground for granting such recognition."

Chapter 32

SOUTH KOREA

1. Under general law

The South Korean legal system is based on civil law. Most of the laws are codified but unwritten customary law and practice may be applied if there is a lacuna in the written law.

There is no apparent limitation to the rights of a foreign creditor or a foreign administrator to bring actions in the Korean courts. A foreign judgment or order may be enforced in Korea by petitioning a Korean court for an enforcement judgment, at which stage the court will determine whether the foreign judgment is enforceable in Korea.

The pre-requisites set out in the Korean Code of Civil Procedure (CCP), article 203, must be satisfied for a judgment or order to be enforced. These are as follows:

- the foreign court must have jurisdiction to make the order;
- the judgment or order must be final;
- the Korean defendant must have been properly served with the judgment or order or must have appeared in the foreign court indicating that he had been so served;
- the foreign judgment or order must not offend public policy or good morals; and
- most importantly, there must be reciprocity.

The provisions of the CCP governing the recognition and enforcement of foreign judgments (including foreign insolvency orders) are quite stringent. However, there appears to be a growing trend in Korea towards adopting a more flexible approach when foreign judgments are sought to be recognised and enforced.

The practice of the courts is to enforce judgments and orders provided that the reciprocity of the foreign court is equal to, or more generous than, the corresponding Korean reciprocity. Recent decisions of the lower courts in Korea have indicated that Korean judges wish to see roughly equivalent treatment of Korean judgments in the country of the foreign administration.

When a foreign judgment is recognised by a Korean court, it is considered to have *res judicata* effect. As a result, subsequent proceedings on the same cause of action in a Korean court will be dismissed without further review of the merits of the case. However, if a subsequent action on a different claim, but dependent on the foreign judgment is brought, the Korean courts will decide the case in accordance with the foreign judgment. In this case, the foreign judgment will automatically be recognised.

The Korean courts will not recognise or enforce foreign judgments relating to tax or penal matters.

2.   Assisting legislation

There does not appear to be any law that requires a Korean court to aid or be auxiliary to a foreign court or a foreign administrator.

Korea is not a party to any agreements or treaties governing recognition or enforcement of foreign judgments.

3.   Insolvency practice

A foreign insolvency appears to have a limited effect on a Korean or his assets situate in Korea.

Under the Bankruptcy Act (the Act), article 2, the recognition of a foreign administrator will depend on whether a Korean administrator would be recognised under the laws of the foreign country.

According to the Act, article 3(2), however, a foreign insolvency order has no direct impact on property in Korea. However, if a foreign insolvency order has been made when a petition for the insolvency of the same debtor is presented to the Korean court, the foreign Court's order is prima facie evidence of the debtor's bankruptcy and the Korean court requires no further proof.

The Corporate Reorganisation Act (No 1214, 12 February 1962), article 4 has a similar provision to the Act, article 3(2) under which a reorganisation procedure initiated in a foreign country has no effect in Korea. The Composition Act (No 997, 20 January 1962), article 11, contains a similar provision regarding foreign composition procedures.

Territoriality also applies to Korean proceedings and an insolvency order made by a Korean court will affect only the bankrupt's Korean property.

If a foreign creditor initiates insolvency proceedings in a Korean court or files a claim in local insolvency proceedings, he must submit proof of his citizenship and his legal rights under his own country's law. In addition, he must show that the provisions of his own country's law are the same as under Korean law.

4. Examples

None available.

Chapter 33

SPAIN

1. Under general law

The *"Ley de Enjuiciamiento Civil"* Civil Procedural Act (CPA) 1881, sections 951–958, governs the enforcement of foreign orders and judgments. A foreign judgment will be recognised and have effect in Spain where:

- there is an international treaty between the country where the order was made and Spain (although bankruptcy orders are excluded from the scope of all treaties to which Spain is a signatory); or
- reciprocity is established.

The CPA, section 952, establishes the reciprocity rule. The recognition of a foreign order in Spain will be subject to the same requirements as those imposed in the country where the order was made for the recognition of Spanish orders. The onus of proving reciprocity rests with the applicant.

The CPA, section 953 requires that for a foreign bankruptcy order to be enforced:

- it must be a final judgment in an action *in personam*;
- it must not be a judgment in default or be in contempt of court;
- the order must be based on an obligation which would be enforceable in Spain; and
- it must fulfil the requirements to be considered authentic in Spain.

The procedure is relatively simple and involves:

- an application to the Supreme Court of Spain for an acknowledgement (an exequatur) that an enforcement order should be made. At the same

time a report is made to the Court, and a report to the Public Prosecutor (Ministerio Fiscal); and
– the order being enforced by a first instance court.

A foreign bankruptcy order will only be effective in Spain if the exequatur procedure is followed, although an exequatur may not be granted if:

– the order relates to a matter where a Spanish court has exclusive jurisdiction;
– it is contrary to public policy;
– there is a pre-existing Spanish order in the same action; or
– decisions of the Spanish court are not recognised in the country where the order was made.

2. Assisting legislation

There is no specific legal provision regarding the recognition of foreign bankruptcy orders.

The CPA envisaged that international treaties would govern such matters although all the bilateral and multilateral treaties to which Spain is a signatory specifically exclude bankruptcy matters. There is no specific provision for bankruptcy proceedings in Spain to be ancillary, or supplemental, to foreign proceedings and bankruptcy proceedings commenced in Spain apply strict territoriality.

A foreign administrator or a foreign creditor is recognised in Spain to initiate proceedings under general Spanish civil law.

3. Insolvency practice

A foreign insolvency order enables a foreign administrator to be recognised as the legal representative of a foreign debtor without the necessity of further proceedings for recognition. His *locus standi* will be recognised although he may not take protective or administrative measures in respect of Spanish real property.

Strict territoriality is the basis of Spanish insolvency law. A Spanish court will not decline international jurisdiction in favour of a foreign court and the existence of foreign insolvency proceedings will not prevent Spanish insolvency proceedings being commenced.

A foreign creditor who obtains execution against a Spanish bankrupt and recovers monies to satisfy the indebtedness, will not be obliged under Spanish law to refund those monies to a foreign administrator. Neither is there any obligation to refund the proceeds of a foreign execution to a Spanish administrator.

4. Examples

Minerva del Moncayo (Jurisprudencia Civil 1912, number 26)

Minerva del Moncayo was a Public Limited Company, incorporated under Belgian law with its registered office in Brussels. It owned mines in Soria and Aragón, and was declared bankrupt by the Soria Court of First Instance. Amongst the creditors were 35 Spaniards and 33 foreigners. The Supreme Court upheld the international competence of the Spanish courts to declare such bankruptcy, notwithstanding the domicile of the company's registered office, (the Civil Procedural Act 1881, articles 51 and 70 and the Commercial Code, article 15). The following circumstances were relevant:

- the company had previously requested and obtained from the Spanish court a suspension of payments order;
- the assets consisted of real property situated in Spanish territory;
- the majority of the creditors were Spanish and Spain had been the centre of its commercial operations; and
- there was no indication that any foreign creditor had petitioned for bankruptcy in Brussels and there was no plurality of proceedings.

Artola Hermanos Jurisprudencia Civil, 1894, number 154

Trustees in bankruptcy of the company Artola Hermanos were appointed by the Commercial Court of Sena, France in 1889. Artola Hermanos was a general commercial partnership, with its registered office in Paris, incorporated under French law and consisting of Spaniards. The trustees brought an action for ownership of a copper and cobalt mine in the province of León, which appeared in the assets of the balance sheet presented before the French court. The Supreme Court dismissed their application because they did not obtain an exequatur.

La Barcelona Traction Light and Power Co, Ltd

This company was incorporated in Canada in 1911, and had its registered office in Toronto. Subsidiary companies controlled the hydroelectric industry in Catalonia, Spain. From 1936, with the outbreak of the civil war, La Barcelona stopped paying dividends. In 1945, it undertook to pay part but the Spanish Government did not authorise the transfer of £3 million. On the petition of three shareholders with bonds valued at £11,500, it was declared bankrupt by the Court of Renus on 12 February 1948.

The Belgian Government, with whose nationals no out-of-court settlement was reached, sued the Spanish Government before the International Court of

Justice. The Spanish Government and the Belgian Government accepted the application of Spanish insolvency law, but they argued over the application of the Spanish law. The Belgian Government argued that adjudication of bankruptcy was only possible under Spanish law in the event of insolvency. The Spanish Government argued cessation of payments was sufficient. The Court of the Hague did not hear the merits of the action but ruled that the Belgian Government did not have *locus standi* to intervene.

Chapter 34

SWEDEN

1. Under general law

Foreign judgments including foreign bankruptcy judgments are not normally recognised or enforceable in Sweden without an order of the Swedish court. If a creditor or a foreign administrator wishes to gain access to property in Sweden, he must first obtain a Swedish judgment by issuing proceedings there.

The exceptions to this general rule are as follows:

- where the foreign creditor is from a country which is a party to a convention with Sweden; and
- where the contract between the disputing parties determines the court which will adjudicate the dispute.

The Swedish Code of Judicial Procedure 1942, section 1, sets out rules for determining the competent court. This will be determined by reference to any of the following:

- the place where the debtor habitually resides
- the debtor's place of administration
- the place where the debtor is physically present; or
- if the debtor is a Swedish national who is abroad, he may be sued in the court of the place where he last resided in Sweden.

Alternatively, proceedings may be brought where assets are located in Sweden. The presence of any assets belonging to a debtor is sufficient to enable a Swedish court to find jurisdiction notwithstanding that the assets may be of minimal value only.

A foreign claimant who is not exempt by any convention or regulation and who commences legal proceedings in Sweden may have to provide security in the form of a guarantee or bond if the debtor applies for security. Nationals of the following are exempt from these provisions:

- Denmark, Iceland and Japan;
- Member States of the Hague Conventions of 17 July 1905 and 1 March 1954; and
- Member States of the New York Convention of 20 June 1956.

There is specific legal provision for the recognition and enforcement of some judgments of the Swiss courts. A special exequatur must be obtained from the Svea Court of Appeal and following that an application for enforcement proceedings can be made. (It is unclear whether this includes bankruptcy proceedings of any form.)

2.   Assisting legislation

The only specific assisting legislation is for the Nordic Multilateral Bankruptcy Convention of 7 November 1933. The signatories are Denmark, Finland, Iceland, Norway and Sweden.

The Convention provides for full recognition in all contracting countries of domestic bankruptcies opened in any contracting state.

Insolvency proceedings commenced in a signatory country include assets in all signatory countries. However, proceedings in one country do not prevent the continuation of insolvency proceedings in another country if such proceedings had been commenced earlier. In this instance, there are no rules concerning the co-operation between the two administrations. However, where insolvency proceedings are commenced in a signatory country, the Convention determines the assistance that should be given by the Courts in the other Nordic countries.

No special exequatur is required and questions of law are referred to the courts of the state where insolvency proceedings were opened, save for issues involving preferences or securities which are resolved by the law of the state where the assets are situated.

Because of the close relationship between the contracting states, this bankruptcy Convention is probably the most sophisticated multilateral agreement in the world at present. It appears to work smoothly but there is little case law (possibly indicating few disputes) and there are few complicating factors.

There are no specific provisions governing bankruptcy jurisdiction; it is governed by Swedish civil law. The Swedish Bankruptcy Act (*Konkurslagen*) number 670 of 1987 Chapter 2, section 1, provides that a bankruptcy application must be filed with the court where the debtor can in general be sued for a debt. A similar rule for compositions is set out in the Compositions Act (*Ackordslagen*) number 847 of 1970.

3. Insolvency practice

Principles of strict territoriality apply when there are foreign insolvency proceedings and the country concerned is not a signatory to the Nordic Multilateral Bankruptcy Convention. The foreign insolvency proceedings will, in principle, be ignored. Foreign insolvency proceedings will not prevent domestic insolvency proceedings being commenced. The bankruptcy code does not contain reference to foreign proceedings and is based on the principle of territoriality for foreign insolvencies and universality for domestic insolvencies.

A foreign bankrupt estate is capable of having rights and obligations and can sue and be sued in Sweden, but the bankruptcy does not affect assets located in Sweden which remain at the disposal of the debtor. A foreign administrator has no power to deal with the debtor's assets in Sweden and proceedings for attachments, judgments, executions or even local bankruptcy in Sweden are still possible. The justification for this is apparently protection of Swedish creditors but it may also be used by foreign creditors irrespective of whether or not they have proved in the foreign bankruptcy. Any surplus in the Swedish insolvency is not paid to a foreign administrator but to the debtor himself.

In a Swedish domestic insolvency, the foreign administrator will depend on foreign procedural law where assets are situated in other jurisdictions. The present interpretation of Swedish law is that the debtor is obliged to co-operate with his office holder to collect foreign assets. This is based on the Swedish Penal Code which makes it a crime for a debtor to withhold assets from a Swedish administrator. This can be enforced by granting powers of attorney in favour of the administrator or by a transfer of ownership to the administrator.

The nationality or residence of a creditor is irrelevant for the purposes of Swedish insolvency jurisdiction: all creditors participate equally if their claims are enforceable in Sweden. Recoveries abroad are taken into consideration when calculating dividends and, in this instance, excess monies can be reclaimed from the creditor. Where there are parallel foreign and Swedish bankruptcy proceedings, the Swedish administrator will take into account receipts by creditors in other proceedings.

4. Examples

Case 1

A Swedish administrator sold a yacht in Italy which belonged to a bankrupt. The proceeds of sale were due to be transferred from the Italian buyer to the administrator in Sweden. A broker obtained an attachment of the proceeds stating he was entitled to commission. The Swedish administrator was advised that he would find it difficult to vacate the attachment made by the Italian court since Italian law provides that all disputes initiating from bankruptcy should be handled by the bankruptcy court, which was the District Court of Stockholm. However, the Swedish administrator could not bring an action in the Swedish courts since the assets were in Italy and the court was not competent. This case was settled.

Case 2

This case is an example of the practical problems of obtaining information and bringing proceedings abroad. A Swedish individual was declared bankrupt but managed to leave Sweden and when traced was living in luxury in Florida, United States. It was thought that a substantial amount of money and antiques had been taken by the bankrupt when she left Sweden. The Swedish administrator sought to issue proceedings in a local American court to recover the assets and obtain information about her whereabouts and the extent of her assets. An order for extradition was obtained through diplomatic channels and the bankrupt was jailed until she could be returned to Sweden, but by this time her assets had been dissipated.

Case 3

A Swedish bankrupt owned shares in a Swiss company. The bankrupt refused to give a power of attorney and the company refused to act on the authority of the Swedish administrator without written instructions from the bankrupt. A settlement was reached eventually.

Case 4

A Swedish administrator sought recovery of assets from Belgium. The bankrupt successfully argued that the request of the Swedish administrator could not be granted as Belgian law requires reciprocity and a Swedish court would not recognise the same request from a Belgian administrator.

Cunard 773F. 2d 452 (2nd CIR 1985)

A Swedish shipping company was declared bankrupt in Sweden. A British creditor obtained an attachment order on a debt due to the Swedish company by an American debtor. The British creditor argued that the United States Bankruptcy Code, section 304 was the exclusive remedy of an administrator who wished to stay or enjoin creditors actions in the United States. The United States court vacated the attachment on the basis of comity to the Swedish courts. This was confirmed by the Court of Appeal. Whilst reciprocity is a factor to be considered, it is not a condition precedent to the granting of comity.

Banque de Commerce de l'Azow-Don v *Stockholms and Enskilda Bank (NJA 1945)*

A Russian bank was declared bankrupt by a French court. The court based juris-diction on the presence of the directors carrying on business activities in France. The French bankrupt estate sued a Swedish bank in Sweden for the recovery of assets which had been deposited in Sweden before confiscation. The Swedish bank claimed that the French bankrupt estate had no *locus standi* since its authority was territorially limited to France. The Supreme Court of Stockholm held that the French bankrupt estate could be a party to judicial proceedings in Sweden since it had legal capacity according to French law. However, the French bankruptcy could not affect the administration of the bankrupt's property in Sweden which did not belong to the French estate and consequently could not be claimed by it.

Chapter 35

SWITZERLAND

1. Under general law

The underlying concept of the recognition of foreign insolvency orders and foreign administrators in Switzerland is territorial but one of "judicial assistance". Swiss insolvency proceedings may be commenced in respect of an insolvent debtor but the liquidation process including the realisation of the debtor's estate will be administered only by the Swiss authorities and only according to Swiss law. Any surplus will be paid to the foreign administrator.

Swiss law also requires reciprocity. At present the Swiss courts consider that Belgium, Germany, France, Luxembourg and, possibly, Greece, Italy and Spain offer reciprocity to Swiss insolvency proceedings. Partial reciprocity is considered given by the United Kingdom, Canada, the United States and Australia.

No reciprocity appears to be recognised in respect of the Netherlands, Portugal, Japan, Denmark, Finland, Sweden, Norway, Austria or Liechtenstein.

2. Assisting legislation

The Swiss Federal Statute on Private International Law (PILS), articles 166–175 enforced on 1 January 1989, governs the recognition in Switzerland of foreign insolvency proceedings, including bankruptcies, foreign compositions and arrangements.

A foreign administrator, or a creditor in the foreign bankruptcy, may apply for the recognition of the foreign bankruptcy order and this shall be recognised pursuant to PILS, article 166 provided that:

 – the bankruptcy order is enforceable in its country of origin;
 – certain minimal procedural requirements have been complied with;
 – there is reciprocity;

- it does not conflict with Swiss public policy; and
- the foreign court has jurisdiction to declare the debtor bankrupt according to Swiss law *i.e.* the bankrupt was resident or had its seat in the foreign country.

An application for recognition should be addressed to the relevant court where the assets sought are located.

In addition, an order for protective measures can be sought prior to seeking the recognition of the bankruptcy order. If assets are spread throughout Switzerland, the first court to which an application is made will consider the question of recognition and will have jurisdiction in respect of all assets situate in Switzerland.

The competent court is usually determined by Cantonal law which also governs the relevant procedure. Whether the debtor is entitled to be heard prior to the court deciding on recognition is also governed by Cantonal law.

Once a Swiss judgment has been issued confirming the recognition of the foreign bankruptcy order, that order has the same effect as a Swiss bankruptcy order. Effectively, the bankrupt's assets over the legally protected minimum vest in the local insolvency authority, and the debtor is obliged to disclose the whereabouts of all assets to the Swiss administrator.

The Swiss administrator is required to notify the time by which claims against the debtor must be filed. There are four categories of preference established by the Swiss Federal Law on Debt Collection and Bankruptcy of 1889 (LDCB), article 219 and Swiss assets will be realised pursuant to the rules set out in the LDCB and the creditors paid accordingly. If a creditor's claim does not fall into one of these four categories, the creditor cannot claim in the Swiss administration.

Any surplus will be paid to the foreign administrator provided that the Swiss court which recognised the foreign bankruptcy order decides that the conduct of the foreign proceedings is in accordance with Swiss procedural fairness. The treatment of Swiss creditors in the foreign insolvency proceedings will be considered and these creditors have a right to be heard by the Swiss court prior to the surplus being paid to the foreign administrator. If the Swiss court considers the foreign treatment of Swiss claims to be unacceptable under Swiss law, the surplus will be paid to unsecured creditors in Switzerland.

The PILS, article 175 provides that where there has been an agreement with creditors or some other form of reorganisation ratified by a foreign court, that agreement will be recognised in Switzerland and PILS, articles 166–170 will apply.

3. Insolvency practice

The foreign administrator should submit details of the foreign insolvency proceedings and the assets claimed to the Swiss courts as soon as possible. If the details are not placed before the court or if the court does not recognise the foreign proceedings, any excess assets after payment of secured and preferential claims will be used to pay Swiss unsecured creditors, rather than the foreign administrator.

The Swiss courts do not appear to have considered whether foreign insolvency proceedings would be recognised if no formal application was made to commence Swiss insolvency proceedings; for example, in a case where there were no Swiss assets. On the basis of current case law, it appears that the foreign insolvency proceedings would not be recognised.

The most effective method for a foreign creditor or foreign administrator to pursue a debt or debts in Switzerland without commencing Swiss bankruptcy proceedings is to attach the debtor's assets. This can only be granted if there is a private law monetary claim against a debtor. In addition, one of the grounds for obtaining an attachment must be proved, for example:

– the debtor has no domicile, or place of business where a writ of execution could be levied; or
– there is evidence that the debtor is recovering assets from Switzerland.

The risk is that the applicant may be liable for damages if the attachment is unjustified. The extent to which a creditor can attach assets in Switzerland after a debtor is declared bankrupt abroad, but before the bankruptcy order is recognised in Switzerland, is uncertain.

4. Examples

None available.

Chapter 36

UNITED STATES OF AMERICA

1. Under general law

United States of America (US) courts are generally inclined to recognise judgments or orders of foreign courts pursuant to the doctrine of comity. There is a general presumption in favour of comity in that the party objecting to the enforcement of a foreign order bears the burden of proving impropriety or unfairness in the foreign action. There are a number of procedures which enable foreign claimants to pursue a US defendant including:

- Both State and Federal Courts recognise foreign judgments under the doctrine of comity. Foreign claimants with judgments in their own courts against US defendants may petition the State Court, or the Federal Court in the state where the defendants reside or carry on business, to recognise the foreign judgments and issue its own orders for enforcement;
- Most US states have adopted the Uniform Foreign Money Judgments Recognition Act (UFMJRA) which sets out rules for the recognition and enforcement of foreign money judgments. These are generally enforceable in both State and Federal Courts. The US courts must be satisfied that the enforcement of the foreign judgment is fundamentally fair. They will not enforce a judgment if it appears that the foreign court did not have jurisdiction to give judgment in that matter, the judgment was procured by fraud, the defendant did not have sufficient time to defend the proceedings, or enforcement would violate US public policy; or
- In the absence of a foreign judgment, it is also possible for foreign claimants to commence original proceedings against a US defendant in the State Court or the Federal Court where the defendant resides or carries on business, pursuant to the doctrine of comity. This is limited slightly by the requirement in some states that the foreign claimant may need to be registered as doing business in the state prior to initiating proceedings.

The reason for this is that, by registering with the state, the foreign claimant is acknowledging that it is subject to suit in that state, and some states believe that as a matter of policy, a foreign claimant should not have access to their courts unless the claimants themselves can be sued in such courts. The matter will be adjudged on its merits and the final judgment of the court will be enforceable anywhere in the US.

2. Assisting legislation

The US has uniform federal bankruptcy legislation in the form of the US Bankruptcy Code (the Code), and all bankruptcy cases are adjudged by the specialised Federal Bankruptcy Courts. There are several provisions of the Code dealing with assistance to foreign administrators and foreign insolvency proceedings, primarily sections 303, 304, 305 and 306 of the Code. The Code is not the exclusive remedy for foreign administrators, and they are free to pursue assistance in the State and non-bankruptcy Federal Courts pursuant to the doctrine of comity as discussed above.

Section 304(a) authorises a foreign administrator to commence proceedings ancillary to foreign insolvency proceedings. The latter must be administrative or judicial and recent case law indicates that the foreign debtor (individual or company) need not be eligible for bankruptcy relief in the US for the foreign administrator to commence proceedings under section 304.

Section 304(c) sets out guidelines to be followed by the Bankruptcy Court in assessing the request for recognition and assistance. Generally the courts will be guided by what will best assure the economical and expeditious administration of the insolvent estate provided this is consistent with:

- the just treatment of all the claimants;
- the protection of a US claimant against the inconvenience and prejudice of processing his claim in foreign proceedings;
- the prevention of preferences and fraudulent transactions;
- the distribution of the proceeds of the estate substantially in accordance with the order set out in the Code;
- comity; and
- if appropriate, a fresh start for the foreign insolvent entity.

The foreign administrator files a petition for relief under section 304(a) setting out the background, the capacities of the parties, the relief requested and the reasons why the relief should be granted. Once the petition has been filed, a summons is issued and both the summons and the petition served on interested parties. If no objections are filed, the relief will be granted. If there are objections either a status conference of the interested parties with the judge will be organised or a trial date set.

The relief likely to be granted by the court pursuant to section 304(a) includes orders to:

- enjoin the commencement or continuation of an action against a debtor or his property;
- enforce any judgment against the debtor; or
- turn over property or its proceeds to a foreign administrator.

Section 303(b)4 of the Code enables a foreign administrator to file an involuntary bankruptcy petition against the foreign debtor under Chapter 7 (Liquidation) or Chapter 11 (Reorganisation) with the Bankruptcy Court. For this, the debtor must have either its residence, domicile, place of business or property in the US. If the involuntary petition is not contested or is granted after trial, the debtor will be subject to full, primary US insolvency proceedings under the relevant Chapter of the Code.

Section 305 of the Code permits a Bankruptcy Court to dismiss or suspend any pending US insolvency proceedings if there currently exists foreign insolvency proceedings with respect to the debtor and the factors listed in section 304(c) warrant such dismissal or suspension.

Section 306 of the Code provides that the appearance in the Bankruptcy Court by a foreign administrator in connection with a petition or request under sections 303, 304 or 305 does not submit the foreign administrator to the jurisdiction of any US court for any purpose other than such petition or request, but the Bankruptcy Court may condition the granting of such petition or request on compliance by the foreign administrator with the Bankruptcy Court's orders.

3. Insolvency practice

A foreign administrator must prove that he has the capacity to maintain an action and may:

- commence ancillary proceedings pursuant to section 304(a);
- commence full bankruptcy proceedings pursuant to section 303(b)(4);
- obtain a judgment in the foreign jurisdiction which will be recognised and enforced in the US pursuant to either the Uniform Money Judgments Recognition Act, in the case of a money judgment, or generally under the doctrine of comity; or
- commence an action in the US under the doctrine of comity in which he will be recognised by the State and Federal Courts.

In practice, the Bankruptcy Courts and the other State and Federal Courts have a wide discretion in granting relief or recognition in accordance with the above.

The issues recurring in US case law are:

- the foreign court must have personal and subject matter jurisdiction;
- there must be procedural fairness in the foreign insolvency proceedings. Fairness will be assumed by the courts unless there is evidence to the contrary. As a matter of public policy, the more the foreign legal system differs from the US system, the more difficult it will be to show that it was fair; and
- the relief granted must not violate public policy.

4.   Examples

Hilton v Guyot, 159 U S 113 (1895)

One of the first comity cases involving the recognition of a French judgment against a US citizen who was conducting business in France.

Cunard Steamship Co v Salen Reefer Servs, 773 F 2d 452 (2d Cir 1985)

Federal non-bankruptcy case confirming that US Bankruptcy Code, section 304 is not the exclusive remedy for a foreign administrator.

In re Gee, 53 Bankr, 891 (Bankr. S.D.N.Y. 1985) ; *In re Culmer,* 25 Bankr, 621 (Bankr, S.D.N.Y. 1982)

Leading cases granting access and recognition pursuant to US Bankruptcy Code, section 304.

In re Maxwell Communication Corp plc, 170 B.R. 800 (Bankr. S.D.N.Y. 1994) ; *In re Axona Int'l Credit & Commerce, Ltd,* 88 B.R. 597 (Bankr. S.D.N.Y. 1988) aff'd 115 B.R. 442 (S.D.N.Y. 1990) *appeal dismissed, 924 F.2d 31 (2d Cir. 1991)*

Leading cases involving full US insolvency cases under Chapter 11 (*Maxwell*) and Chapter 7 (*Axona*) with respect to foreign debtors concurrently subject to foreign insolvency proceedings.